DES PAWSON'S
KNOT CRAFT
& ROPE MATS

This book is dedicated to those forgotten and anonymous sailors, riggers, sailmakers, fendermakers and other workers with rope who passed their knowledge on to the next generation so these skills can be with us today. Thank you.

Adlard Coles Nautical
An imprint of Bloomsbury Publishing Plc

50 Bedford Square	29 Earlsfort Terrace	1385 Broadway
London	Dublin 2	New York
WC1B 3DP	Ireland	NY 10018
UK		USA

www.bloomsbury.com
www.adlardcoles.com

ADLARD COLES, ADLARD COLES NAUTICAL and the Buoy logo
are trademarks of Bloomsbury Publishing Plc

First published 2016
© Des Pawson, 2016

Des Pawson has asserted his right under the Copyright, Designs
and Patents Act, 1988, to be identified as Author of this work.

British Library Cataloguing-in-Publication Data
A catalogue record for this book is available from the British Library.

Library of Congress Cataloguing-in-Publication data has been applied for.

ISBN:	PB:	978-1-4729-2278-6
	ePDF:	978-1-4729-2280-9
	ePub:	978-1-4729-2279-3

8 10 9

Typeset in 10 pt Haarlemmer MT
Typesetting and page layout by Gridlock Design
Printed and bound in India by Replika Press Pvt Ltd

To find out more about our authors and books visit www.bloomsbury.com. Here you will find extracts,
author interviews, details of forthcoming events and the option to sign up for our newsletters.

Photographs © Horst A. Friedrichs

DES PAWSON'S KNOT CRAFT & ROPE MATS

60 Ropework Projects Including 20 Mat Designs

ADLARD COLES NAUTICAL

BLOOMSBURY

LONDON · OXFORD · NEW YORK · NEW DELHI · SYDNEY

Contents

Introduction

Many people ask me if I have an apprentice; the answer is 'no', but by sharing my knowledge in print I hope to help many more than I might by having an apprentice. In the first place I learned my trade from books; the beauty of books is that they can be referred to long after a one-to-one lesson has finished. In some ways it can be said that I learned from many masters, and although some are no longer with us, their thoughts and expertise endure in their writings. This book, born from a wish to build on my previous published book, *Des Pawson's Knot Craft*, contains more projects and many more mats, both of which I have been asked for by a lot of people.

I find that drawings are the best vehicle to explain what is going on in a particular knot or sennit. Learning to 'read' the drawings is in itself a skill to be gained; do not start with the most complicated thing. Indeed, if possible try to equate one diagram with a knot you already know; in that way you will gain an understanding of the visual language used in this book. The use of colour in the diagrams I hope makes them a little clearer.

Many books have been published on how to tie practical knots, and a lesser number on decorative knotting. While the latter may show how to make a fancy knot, they don't provide much help in putting the knots together to make an object – be it a key fob, fender, rope ladder, mat or lanyard. Sometimes there may be an illustration of a finished item for inspiration, or even a couple of extra projects, but rarely is there a step-by-step breakdown, complete with details of the exact size and lengths of materials required and with full instructions – the complete recipe for the very thing you want to make. Here, I hope, is the book that provides just that.

Not having enough cordage is a continual risk. However much you try to remember how much line went into an item you have made in the past, you have long since forgotten and you are back to guessing, hoping that you have guessed correctly or with a bit to spare. Then comes the day when you have a length of good old rope and you want to make a mat with it; the length is tight – if only you knew the exact amount needed. Or you have six metres of super-fine tarred 3mm twine left. Will this be enough for that bell rope you wanted to make as a special gift, or having started will you find it's too short and the six metres wasted? The wasting of rope, new or old, is something that any owner, skipper, mate, bosun or craftsman abhors. Cordage is a precious material to be valued, treasured and conserved.

After many years of guesswork and the occasional note in the margins of my knotting books, I belatedly, in 1977, started to keep a 'recipe book'. In this I recorded the finished size of the item I had made, what material I had used, and how much had been needed to make it. I added the special little tricks and hints that helped the item to fall right and to be finished neatly. I sketched the special knot that was required, or noted the book that gave this information. I was able to add special details and methods shown to me by my knotting peers. And while inevitably not everything always got recorded, over the years I have built up a great body of information.

Rope makes wonderful hard-wearing mats. You can use old rope, new rope or even the yarns drawn out from old rope and plaited together. Historically such mats would have been used as doormats and to protect against chafe on ships. Today they can give a boat a real seamanlike touch. Around the home there are few things nicer than a home-made doormat, while smaller mats can serve as coasters or table mats, to protect a table from a hot pan, stand a plant pot or vase on, or perhaps set off an antique model boat. You could even make mats in fine twine for a doll's house (a good way of practising without using a great deal of material!). I have included a wide selection of designs, ranging from the very simple basic flattened Turk's head to the most complex and challenging interlinked hitches, or a mat with many bights on each side.

Within these pages I share with you a selection of the designs and ideas from my recipe book. When demonstrating, I am often asked how to make the various things that I have around me, so here are the basic designs, an indication of their size and details of which knots and sennits are used to make them. I give you a list of materials and their lengths and sizes – and in specifying the lengths I have erred very slightly on the side of generosity because all materials vary in the way they make up, and each craftsman's knotting tension differs. You may well wish to adjust the material lengths to suit yourself and your favourite cordage. The stated materials and knots should make what I describe, but it is always possible to make items longer or shorter, or to use bigger or smaller line. It can help to keep a record of any variations: the more information you have, the better your guesses will be in the future.

As this is a recipe book rather than a how-to-tie-knots book (there is a good list of these on page 170), I have simply named the knots and sennits that go to make up each item. This can lead to a degree of misunderstanding, as many knots have more than one name, so in most cases there is a simple aide-memoire for the more specialised knots or techniques. Rather than each of these being repeated every time it crops up in a design, there is a cross-reference to the page with the illustration.

These are my projects, the knots put together in the way I prefer, yet there is no reason you should not mix and match to create your own designs. Indeed I would encourage you to experiment. Cordage is a versatile medium, and a joy to use for creating all sorts of things. My aim is to give you the confidence to start making things with knots; this is the book that will make other knot books work for you.

Happy knotting,

Des Pawson

Some tips *of the trade*

During my years of working with rope I have come across pieces of information, special solutions, tools and techniques from many sources that have in some way been of significant help or interest, and I would like to pass on as many of these as I can.

> ### ∾ Concentration ∾
>
> You cannot make good work when watching the television! Take things slowly, making sure each layer of your work looks good, neat and symmetrical. If in doubt, tighten round again until it is, as a poorly tied section will stand out.

TOOLS

HEAVING MALLET

This sadly neglected tool is a great help in pulling tight stubborn strands in a large rope splice, for tightening seizings, and anywhere else that an extra bit of pull is needed. It works best with a heaving board to pull/heave against.

HEAVER

When I was in Mariehamn, the rigger on the Pommern, known as 'Little Brother', showed me a heaver made from a piece of metal pipe with a slot at one end and holes at the other. The strand, or line, is put in the slot and a spike put through the hole; the tool is then turned like a key to tighten the strand or line.

MARLINESPIKE

Look for a good long taper on your marlinespike. I prefer a rounded, flattened point. As with all tools it is rare that a brand new tool is perfect, so it is well worth the trouble to smooth and adjust the shape to your own ideal.

If you are going to use your marlinespike aloft then ensure there is a hole so that you can fit a lanyard.

SWEDISH FID

The tool that makes my living for me is the Swedish fid, so called because the original was patented by a Swede, AJ Svenson, in 1953. It comes in a number of sizes. After any sharp edges have been smoothed and

Heaving board (with mallet)

the end nicely rounded, it is a far better tool for most work than the traditional wooden fid. When it is tucked into the rope or knot, it forms a channel for a strand to pass along and the groove means that a better grip is obtained when working a knot tight with its tip.

LOOKING AFTER WOODEN FIDS
Fids are really only stretching tools; they are not levers. Many a wooden fid has had its end broken because it has been used to lever open strands. If there is a need to lever, then use a steel marlinespike to open out the strand first, before pushing the fid well in – you can use a bit of tallow to ease the passage of the tool.

LITTLE MARLINESPIKES
These can be made from a six-inch nail with a sharpened end and a Turk's head round its head. A small sharpened metal meat skewer has been in my ditty bag since I was a boy. A screwdriver can also be shaped up for a makeshift marlinespike.

SIX-INCH NAILS
These are also good for pegging out such items as bowsprit nets and scramble nets on the lawn.

LOOP TOOLS
I have made up loop tools with various lengths and gauges of bent piano wire, which can be obtained from model shops. I have found that the wire centre from Morse cable controls will also work. Short loop tools are good for pulling the ends through on small button knots, while long tools will be of help for splicing braid on braid line and for pulling through the lashing strands when making up the cores for a button fender.

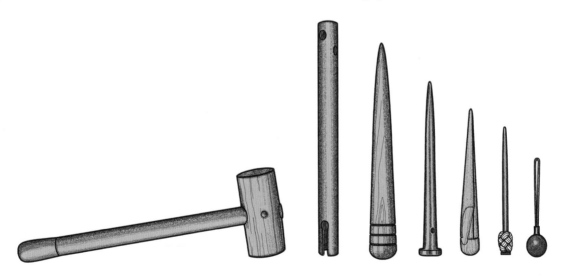

Left to right: Heaving mallet, heaver, fid, marlinespike, Swedish fid, little marlinespike, loop tool

SERVING STICK

A very good replacement for a serving mallet or serving board is a narrow piece of wood in which a series of holes is drilled. The line is threaded through the holes to give the required tension and the serving applied in the normal manner. A very short serving stick will enable you to serve quite small eyes.

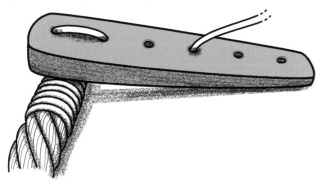

Serving stick

KNIVES

There is much debate about what makes a good knife and what makes a good blade (for example, will it keep a good edge?). Some people are totally against stainless steel, saying that it will never give a good edge.

The first thing to bear in mind is that different tasks require different types of edge. You could never cut a 48mm piece of manila with a cut-throat razor, and if you tried you would ruin the razor forever. I differentiate between the razor-sharp edge I put on my pocket knife and use for cutting and trimming small stuff, and the saw-like edge I put on my bench knives for cutting ropes and cables. I get the razor edge by sharpening it on a softish fine stone, and the saw-like edge by sharpening it with a very coarse stone or a steel.

As far as a lubricant for the stone is concerned (and, of course, there must be a lubricant to stop the pores of the stone clogging up) I use water, but this can only be used if you start with a new piece of stone. If the stone has already been used with oil, I use paraffin (kerosene) with a touch of oil. I believe that a knife will only hold its edge for a long time if it is never used, so a frequent tickle on stone or steel, and not allowing the tool to get into too bad a state, is by far the better practice.

As far as the argument between carbon and stainless steel goes, it is worth remembering that there are many variations of both. I have knives in both materials that

∽ FINGER PROTECTION ∽

Repeatedly pulling fine line tight, when hitching, seizing and whipping, can soon cut into your fingers. After much work you can build up calluses, but if you would prefer not to go through the agony of building them up and if the material is not too sensitive to very slight soiling, cut short lengths of bicycle inner tube to slip over the figures you favour for pulling with. If no inner tube, some tape or a fine leather tube can work as well. If the material is sensitive to soiling, it is best to do modest amounts of work at a time, to help build up some kind of hardening of the fingers.

work for me. Often these are just basic utility knives, as used by butchers or fishermen, but it should be borne in mind that at sea, salt water soon ruins the best of carbon steel knives, unless great care is taken to keep them dry and clean.

KNOTS
Some knots are almost tools in themselves.

CONSTRICTOR KNOT
Works well as a temporary seizing, holding together the end of a rope, a bundle of lines before making

a button knot, building the core of a fender and many other examples. When pulled really tight you may have to cut it to remove it. However, when you understand the structure of the knot it is possible to untie in many circumstances with the help of a fid or spike.

PACKER'S KNOT
Based on the figure of eight, this knot works well when making up such things as fender bases, as the more you pull the tighter it grips. It can be locked with a half hitch, to make it secure.

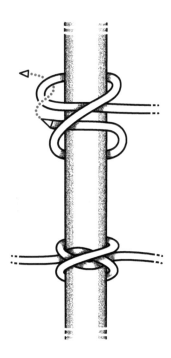

Constrictor knot

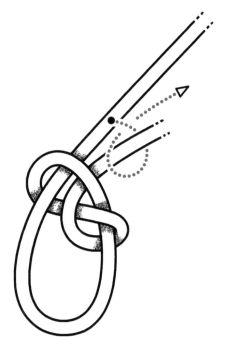

Packer's knot

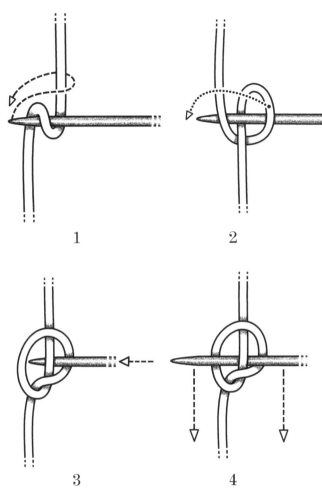

Marlinespike hitch, step by step

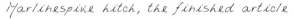

Marlinespike hitch, the finished article

MARLINESPIKE HITCH

The best way of pulling fine line extra tight without cutting your fingers. The direction of pull is important; if you make the knot in the wrong direction or pull in the wrong direction the hitch slips.

BUNDLES

When working with long lengths of line it is helpful to make them up into bundles. There are many ways of doing this, but just wrapping the line round your hand and holding the bundle in place with a rubber band works as well as anything. You should start the wrapping near the work and hank round your hand until you get to the end; with a bit of luck, the line can be pulled out from the centre of the bundle as you work. If things start to get into a mess sort them out and rehank before you have a completely knotted mess of a bundle.

GUNK, GOOS, TAR, ETC.

TALLOW

A touch of tallow on your fid or spike is a great help. It only needs a little. You can make your own tallow by saving the fat from your roast beef or lamb (pork is no good). Put the congealed fat into some water, boil it up and when it has cooled and gone hard, skim it from the top. Repeat once more and this should remove most of the impurities. You will also find that tallow will help clean your hands of Stockholm tar. A blob rubbed into the hand, then wiped off on to a cloth will get rid of most, and then soap and water should do the rest.

LINSEED OIL

This is good for 'feeding' wood and, mixed with Stockholm tar, can be the base for a treatment for rigging. It is worth knowing that there are two types of linseed oil, boiled and raw. The boiled oil will go off and harden almost like paint. Raw oil soaks right in, boiled oil forms a skin.

RIGGING MIXTURES

I do not think that rigging mixes are particularly scientific. Use a mixture of perhaps 2:1 of Stockholm tar to boiled linseed oil, with a touch of dryers if possible, to help it go off. If the tar is very thick and you want it to penetrate into fibres or right into the core of the wire you may wish to add some real turpentine to the mixture. There is no need to add the whiskey described in the recipe given in Brady's Kedge Anchor of 1849:

> *For blacking ship's standing rigging: To half a barrel of tar add six gallons of whiskey, four pounds of litharge, four pounds of lamp black, two buckets of boiling beef pickle or hot salt water out of the coppers, if the other cannot be had conveniently. Mix well together and apply immediately.*

The purpose of any rigging mix is to protect the rope and wire from moisture. Some people paint seizings and servings in a contrasting colour as a decorative feature.

STOCKHOLM TAR

This can still be obtained from tack shops and veterinary sources as it is still used on the hooves of animals.

~ BEESWAX ~

Beeswax, or even candle wax, rubbed on whipping or sewing twine, will make it hold together better and reduce the wear from friction.

PAINTS AND VARNISHES FOR DECORATIVE WORK

In the old days, when only natural materials were used, everything had to be protected from the weather. The quality of the materials may not always have been the best, so paint was used both to protect and to highlight decorative knots, and whole bell ropes would be painted. Ropework on tillers would have been varnished.

If you use natural materials today it is worth remembering this, and you may wish to treat your ropework in the same way. If you have the time and inclination you can do the same on any synthetic lines used. Take care, as varnishes change the colour of materials quite dramatically. Many yacht varnishes

will make a flax or hemp line go very dark brown, like a tarred line, and will turn a white line a golden colour. I have found that some of the varnishes based on either acrylic or PVA (which allow the brushes to be cleaned in water and are sometimes sold as 'low odour') only slightly darken the work. Do some tests first to avoid ruining your work.

MELTED ENDS OF SYNTHETIC ROPE

Do not make great blobs of melted plastic on the ends of your lines; they will crack and, when running through your hands, can do great damage.

If you do decide to melt the ends, do so in a minimal manner, taking care to smooth the end with wetted fingers. Polypropylene has a fairly low melt point and is not too much of a problem if a quick heat is applied, but nylon and polyester have much higher melt points and can burn your fingers very easily. Take care.

∾ USING ADHESIVE TAPE ∾

To make a good quick temporary whipping on working ends, I prefer the clear transparent self-adhesive tape such as Scotch tape, Tessa tape or Sellotape, normally used in the office, to the rather heavier, coloured electric tapes. Modern riggers usually have a reel in a dispenser on their bench. Always work the tape towards the end, winding it on in the same direction as the lay of the rope, thus tightening the twist in the lay. This gives a smooth series of overlaps that are not so likely to catch when pushed through tight spaces. If you want a long pointed end to the rope and you are using three-strand rope, you can taper the end by cutting out first one strand and then a second strand further back, covering the whole with the self-adhesive tape.

MEASURING ROPE

In the past rope was measured by its circumference rather than its diameter, and you can see why when trying to measure a large rope. In the UK and Europe today rope is measured by its diameter in millimetres. As a rough guide you can convert from one to the other by saying that the circumference in eighths of inches is equal to the diameter in millimetres (see conversion table on page 173). It is well worth noting that today in the United States rope is sold by its diameter in inches, but for more than two inches in diameter measurements change over to circumference. Wire rope has always been sold by its diameter, even in the UK.

❧ SIZES AND LENGTHS OF MATERIAL ❧

Material sizes can vary greatly, both from maker to maker and even from batch to batch.

- For larger sizes, especially natural materials, this can easily mean that a piece of rope sold as 24mm could measure 10% larger or even more.

- When worked, rope has a tendency to get shorter and fatter, thus throwing out your calculations.

- Rope measured under slight tension can, in reality, be a lot shorter when you go to work with it.

- Be aware of smaller braided lines: some will have a core, while others have no core, yet be given the same size and description.

- Don't mix material with and without core in the same item.

- If you are buying without actually handling the cordage in question, it can be wise to ask for a sample before committing to buying a lot.

CORDAGE

The right kind of rope for the right job will make all the difference both to the making and to the finished product. I don't come from the school that says natural fibres are best. I think that you should use the appropriate rope for the job. It's worth the trouble searching for the best materials and usually worth paying extra for quality, be it in natural or synthetic material. Good natural materials have a certain feel that is rewarding and can give the item you've made the appearance of coming from the past. But natural materials will rot quite easily and a fine job can soon look very tatty, thus wasting a great deal of work.

It is worth exploring the various imitation natural materials available for jobs that are subject to rot, but even those are not going to last for ever. I like to use a material that is fairly firm and gives good definition to any knots tied in it. If you are splicing it is helpful that the strand itself holds its twist, but you do not need the lay to be so hard as to start to cockle and distort as you splice.

I give some idea as to the sort of material to be used in each of the projects, but you may have to adapt to the materials you can find. This is nothing new, sailors doing fancy knot work 150 years ago would have had to make do with whatever they could lay their hands on.

The source for fine materials can be difficult and you may need to use a number of places to get a variety of materials. Check out the internet. Always try to get a sample before buying for the first time. Some of the companies will only supply in bulk, but it may be worth visiting them if they have the sort of materials you are looking for. Actual rope manufacturers normally only supply in bulk with high minimum orders, but if you have some big projects it may be worth a chat; they can always put you on to one of their stockists.

Farming supply shops or yacht chandlers can also be a good source as, although they may not have natural materials, they may be able to put you on to a good source. Fisherman's stores and co-operatives may also have a good range of interesting materials. Sailmakers and riggers may well sell you short lengths of rope and the odd ball of small stuff. Then there are also a few specialist mail-order suppliers (see Appendices).

Keep your eyes open when travelling and buy when you see the kind of materials you like, laying down like fine wine the best of twines and cord for that special project. Just keep your cordage dry, dust-free and away from insects or other pests and you will bless the day that you bought those special items.

❧ AMOUNT NEEDED ❧

There are lots of things that affect the lengths of cordage a project needs. As well as the size of cordage used and its variation from maker to maker, every person pulls their work tight to a different degree. The more you make items, the tighter your work is likely to become, so if you find yourself short on any of the measurements I have given, allow yourself quite a bit more, certainly for the first time you tackle a new project, and make a note of your usage.

Rope mats can be made open or tighter; this is often a matter of taste. My wife and I tend to like our mats quite close and tight, but others may prefer a more open design, so if in doubt give yourself a bit more for the first attempt.

If you get into trouble with mats you can either, if using three-strand rope, long splice another piece to lengthen your rope or hide a join behind one of the overlaps. But make a note for next time.

∽ PRACTICE AND TEST PIECES, DUMMYING UP ∽

- Some of the more complex multi-strand knots can more easily be understood if you use a small bundle of differently coloured ropes so that each end is a different shade. I have a bundle of 4mm braided line that I find most useful, both to check out exactly what is going on and then, when I understand the basic structure, to see how the whole knot can be modified.

- Making a miniature item before tackling a full size piece can be a useful lesson and help to overcome problems and, at worst, if things go wrong you are not wasting a lot of expensive material.

- When trying to work out how much rope is needed for a variation of a project, say to turn a bell rope into a dog lead, it can be useful to just dummy up a short part, measuring the amount of line used and then calculating what would be needed for the whole.

- Do the same with knots, roughly making up a knot but not working it tight, or only part tucking it, so that you have a guide as to the amount used. If in doubt, add a bit as it is always hard to add extra line into a project and you may finish up by wasting quite a lot of useful material.

KNOT CRAFT

Shackle release lanyard in PORTUGUESE SENNIT

☞ *I was asked to copy this simple but practical lanyard for use as a pull release on certain types of shackle. Note that after two sets of movements the two ends form a reef or square knot. Another name for this sennit is square knotting, and yet another is Solomon's bar. It is the basis of all macramé or, as some sailors used to say, 'McNamara's lace'. Look out for the belt on page 91.*

If just one step is repeated, without the second reverse step, a twist develops in this sennit. That's fine if that's what you want, but you should be the one who decides.

Tied in 3mm or 2mm line and fitted to a split ring, this will also make a fine simple key fob, zip pull or even earrings.

METHOD

❖ Middle the line and hold together about 100mm from the bight. You can do this with your fingers or use a fine piece of twine to make a temporary seizing.

❖ Start the Portuguese sennit as below (decide whether you want it flat or spiral, see below) and continue until you have about a 40mm loop left. The ends can be either trimmed off close and melted to stop them coming undone (mind your fingers) or pulled back inside the sennit alongside the core using a loop of wire or fine line.

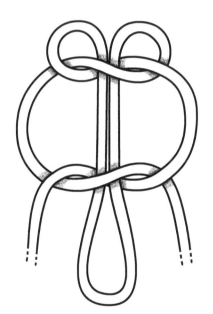

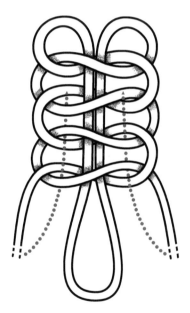

Flat Portuguese sennit, one way of finishing

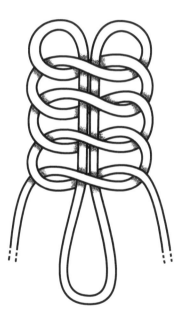

Spiral Portuguese sennit

Portuguese SENNIT BRACELET

☞ *A rope bracelet is easy to make, and can be a nice little gift to give to a special friend. This very basic design leaves plenty of room for variation, be that in the scale of line used, the manner of finishing, using two colours of line, or adding beads or shells at intervals.*

The Portuguese sennit can be flat or spiral (see page 23); furthermore, the spiral sennit could go first in one direction and then in the other. Making such choices is a good way of learning the subtleties.

You could try using a thicker piece of line for the core, in which case allow a little more for the outer line.

Once the principles have been grasped, let your imagination play. Small projects like this can be good for experimenting and learning, so do keep a note of the designs that please you.

MATERIALS

* *For the centre: 600mm of cord*

* *For the outer: 2.2m (if using 1.25mm diameter cord), 2.5m (if using 2mm cord), 3m (if using 3mm cord), maybe a bit more if there is a knot on the end*

KNOTS USED

* *Portuguese sennit – see page 23*

* *Optional: manrope – see page 79, lanyard knot – see pages 126-7*

METHOD

❖ Rather than starting with a single piece of line as in the shackle release lanyard on page 22, start with one strand tied round the bight of a second, giving four ends.

Bracelet start with Portuguese flat sennit

❖ After you have made your Portuguese sennit to whatever length you want, two of the ends can be buried as the finish for the shackle release lanyard and the other two ends used to tie to the initial loop; at a pinch you could get away with just tying off all four ends to the loop.

❖ For a more seamanlike job, all four ends can be finished with a manrope knot or lanyard knot, which will act as a button to close the bracelet.

Simple KEY RING

This combination of the single and then the doubled boatswain's whistle lanyard knot has a simple beauty. I must have made tens of thousands over the years and I am still satisfied each time I make one. As well as being used as a key ring decoration or identifier, it works very well as a shackle release or zip pull, although you may then prefer to make it in 2mm line.

With the addition of the appropriate fitting, a pair will make pretty earrings, green and red will give you port and starboard. Use 3mm for the big earring look, 2mm for a fine look, and if you really want to struggle, work with even smaller line.

At the other end of the scale, tied in something like 6mm line, you will have a basic bell rope, especially if you tie two of the single knots before the doubled knots to make it longer. If you feel up to it, use 24mm or even 36mm rope to make a side fender using just the doubled knot.

I like the name 'boatswain's whistle lanyard knot', but this self-same knot is known by a number of other names: the two-strand diamond knot or sailor's lanyard knot. Whatever name you use, this knot is closely related to the Chinese button knot, said to be the most tied knot in the world; you might believe it when you think of all those Chinese jackets with their knotted buttons.

MATERIALS

* 800mm of 3mm line of your choice

* 25mm or 30mm diameter split ring or key ring

Variations:

* Earring: 600mm of 2mm line, plus the fittings of your choice

* Simple bell rope, two single knots, one double: 2.5m of 6mm

* Side fender of about 250mm diameter: 6.5m of 36mm rope

KNOTS USED

* Boatswain's whistle lanyard knot

* Double boatswain's whistle lanyard knot

METHOD

❖ Fold the line in half, and holding the bight make the single version of the boatswain's whistle lanyard knot, as below.

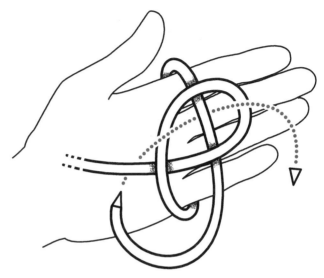

Start of boatswain's whistle lanyard knot

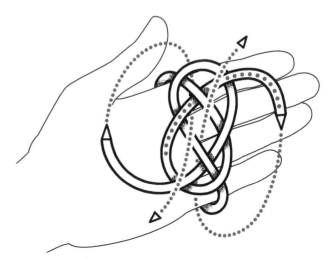

Boatswain's whistle lanyard knot

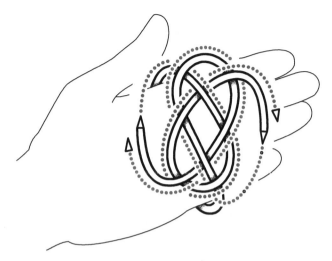

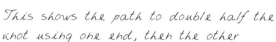

This shows the path to double half the knot using one end, then the other

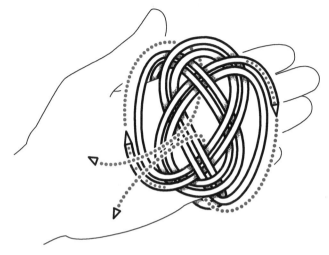

The finish of the doubling and the tucking up through the centre

❖ Tighten so as to leave just a small loop for the split ring, then make a second knot, but this time double it, as below.

❖ Finish the doubling by following round and tucking up through the centre.

❖ Work it up tight, leaving a small space between the single and double knots. Trim the ends with a knife and fit the split ring.

❖ If you are using this as a zip pull, either use a smaller split ring (really small stainless steel split rings can be purchased from an angler's supply shop) or start by threading the line through the hole in the zip tag.

∾ VARIATION: SIDE FENDER ∾

When working with heavy rope to make a side fender you need to allow plenty of rope to tie it loosely first. Then you will need plenty of effort to tighten it, giving quite long ends that need to be trimmed afterwards.

Deluxe KEY RING

☞ *Really a miniature bell rope, this was first put together by my wife Liz. Tied in 3mm as shown, it is very handsome and the star knot is one of the world's almost perfect decorative knots that is not too difficult to tie if you take it one stage at a time. I find this a little bit fiddly to make in 2mm or smaller, but it still looks great.*

By making the body longer and perhaps using 4mm line, you'll have a simple bell rope that will draw admiring remarks from all.

MATERIALS

* 3 × 1m of 3mm line

* 25mm or 30mm split ring

Variation:

* Bell rope, 150mm long: 3 × 2m of 4mm line

KNOTS USED

* Three-strand plait (just like a hair plait) - see page 163

* Temporary seizing, probably a constrictor knot - see page 12

* Three-strand diamond knot or crown and wall knots tied in pairs

* Alternate crown sennit 3+3

* Six-strand star knot - see page 35

* Double crown finish - see page 36

METHOD

❖ Seize the three lengths of line together just off-centre and make a short length of three-strand plait. Fold over and temporarily seize together to make a loop.

❖ Undo any spare plait, arrange the six ends into three sets of two, and make the diamond knot (crown and wall) with these pairs. Work tight up to the loop and remove the temporary seizing.

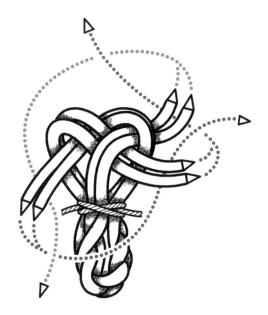

Crown knot followed by wall knot

❖ With every alternate strand make a crown knot, then crown with the remaining three strands. Keep this up until you have about a 40mm length of 3+3 crown sennit, then tie the six-strand star knot.

Tuck all ends up the middle as indicated

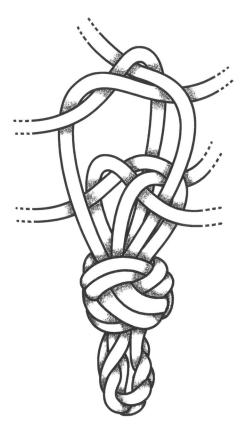

Alternate crown sennit

❖ Work tight and finish with a six-strand crown knot, pulling the ends down through the centre. This little button on the end is called a doubled crown (see page 36).

❖ Finish by trimming the ends close to the base of the star knot.

PYRAMID *key ring*

☞ *An interesting way to make key rings and bell ropes increase gradually in diameter was shown to me by George Payne from Cornwall. He used a crown sennit and added two extra pieces of line across the centre of the crown knot, holding them in place with one more round of crowning, before using the extra four ends with the previous ends to make more crown knots. He continued this process of adding extra pieces of line as he built up the item.*

I had a customer who wanted a key ring a little different to my standard designs, so I gave it a go, starting off as small as I could with what I call a flat crown knot start and then gradually adding two extra ends, so as to change from single-strand crowning to double and then treble, thus building up the pyramid, finishing it off with a star knot with eight of the ends and losing the other ends, by crowning them in the centre of the star knot and pulling the ends down.

Small experimental key rings like this are a good way of trying out ideas and developing a range of variations you can use when making a bell rope.

If it does not work out how you like it, you have not lost a great deal; but if it works out well, make a note of what and how you made the variation, which is how I can share this one with you.

MATERIALS

* 2 x 1.25m of 3mm cord
* 2 x 1m of 3mm cord
* 2 x 900mm of 3mm cord

KNOTS USED

* Flat crown knot
* Four-strand crown knot – see page 75

METHOD

❖ In the middle of your line, tie the flat crown knot start, as below. Make four four-strand crowns before adding in two extra lines.

❖ Make three four-strand crowns with pairs before adding in yet another two lines to give you four lots of three-strands to crown, twelve ends in all.

❖ At this point leave out four ends (one from each bunch of three) and make a star knot with the other eight, with the spare four sticking up through the middle of the star knot.

❖ The eight-strand star knot will have quite a big space in its middle; do not worry. After tightening as best you can, make the twelve ends sticking up into six pairs and tie the fancy crown (see page 47). This will take a bit of thinking. Study the diagram to ensure you are right.

❖ Make sure the pairs are nice, flat and even after tightening. The twelve ends can now be pulled down through the star knot in the way that the star knot was finished off on the deluxe key ring page (see page 29).

❖ Finish by trimming the ends.

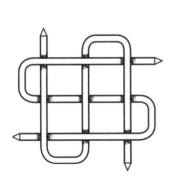

Starting the flat crown knot and adding strands to crowning

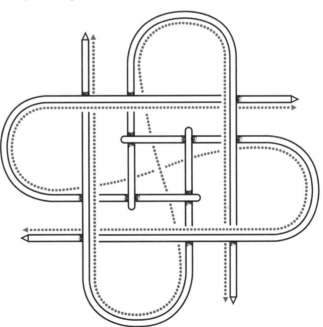

BELL ROPE WORKED WITH SIX ENDS

This is the first commercial bell rope I created, and I am still making it today. I needed money to get married, so to augment my income I made up a couple of samples in some 2mm nylon and took them to the prestigious yacht chandlers in the West End of London, Captain O M Watts. Their buyer looked at my samples, said that they were far too thin, but went on to describe the sort of thing he might be interested in. I went away and made up this design using 3mm cord. That first one took about one and a half hours to make.

This time the buyer liked it, and said he would give me an order. As he wrote down 'Three' in his order book, I thought, 'Is that all, after all this work!' Then he wrote 'dozen'. So, my first order was for thirty-six bell ropes, each taking about an hour and a half; my first introduction to mass production. Practice certainly speeds up the making of any item!

The first main knot, the Matthew Walker knot, is one of my favourites, although it takes quite a bit of time to tie and form into shape. You could, of course, replace it with a quicker knot such as the diamond in pairs that I used at the start of the deluxe key ring (see page 29).

MATERIALS

* 3 x 2m of 3mm line

KNOTS USED

* Three-strand plait (just like a hair plait)

* Temporary seizing, probably a constrictor knot
  - see page 12

* Matthew Walker knot in six strands - see
  page 81

* Alternate crown sennit 3+3 - see page 31

* Diamond knot/crown and wall in six strands -
  see page 72

* Three-strand crown knot - see page 41

* Crown sennit with three pairs - see page 39

* Star knot with six strands

* Double crown finish

METHOD

❖ Start as you would for the deluxe key ring. Seize the three lengths of line together just off centre and make a short length of three-strand plait. Fold over and temporarily seize together to make a loop.

❖ Undo any spare plait, arrange the six ends spread out neatly and separately and, starting with a six-strand wall knot, go on to make a six-strand Matthew Walker.

Star knot start

All strands need to be tucked as shown

❖ Work tight up to the loop and remove the temporary seizing. Now make 45mm of 3+3 crown sennit. Tie with six strands a diamond knot (crown first, then wall below), double this knot and work it tight and even.

❖ With every alternate strand make a three-strand crown knot. Tighten it so that it beds down into the centre of the diamond knot, then go on to make a series of crown knots with three pairs of line, crowning always in the same direction, until you have about 75mm of crown sennit in pairs.

❖ Tie the six-strand star knot. It helps if you see this complex knot as a series of layers, taking it slowly to arrange each layer neatly before moving on to the next one.

Tuck all ends up the middle as indicated

❖ When the star knot has been formed, work it tight systematically one strand at a time. Finish with a doubled crown, as shown below, trimming the ends close to the base of the star knot.

A crown knot doubled by pulling all ends down the middle as shown

❖ If you prefer to finish with a tassel stop at the star knot, just fray out the ends and trim to length. Dunk in very warm water, to help get rid of the kinks in the yarns.

Bell rope WORKED
WITH EIGHT ENDS

👉 *I call this our eleven-inch bell rope, but you can make it longer or shorter, add Turk's heads and interweave colour to change its style. Once you've got the hang of the eight-strand square sennit it grows quite fast, so combined with the crown sennits it makes a long bell rope fairly quickly. The first time it may take you two to three hours to complete… with a bit of luck!*

I usually stop after the eight strands crowned in pairs, but you could add another section with the eight strands crowned singly; this will leave a space in the core of the sennit, so you will need to put in some sort of filler, perhaps a bit of 4/5mm line if you are using 3mm for your sennit.

Sometimes I make up the end globe knot and follow it round a second time, then introduce a second coloured strand for the other. With a three-lead five-bight or four-lead five-bight Turk's head above in the same coloured line, it really makes a deluxe bell rope. Use your imagination to try out all sorts of combinations of the knots and sennits I've used here.

MATERIALS

❋ 4 x 3m of 3mm line

❋ Wooden ball, about 36mm in diameter

❋ Extra lengths of 3mm of a different colour for Turk's heads or interweaving of the globe knot end

KNOTS USED

❋ Four-strand round sennit - see page 74

❋ Diamond knot with four pairs - see page 112

❋ Eight-strand square sennit

❋ Diamond knot/crown and wall with eight strands - see similar on pages 30-1, 72, 112

❋ Alternate crown sennit 4+4 - see page 31

❋ Star knot with eight strands - see page 35

❋ Crown sennit with four pairs

❋ Eight-strand globe knot ball covering

❋ Optional: Turk's heads, three-lead five-bight, for decoration - see page 44

METHOD

❖ Start as the deluxe key ring on page 29, but this time make the loop using four-strand round sennit and the diamond knot with four pairs of line.

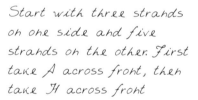

Start with three strands on one side and five strands on the other. First take A across front, then take H across front

Do the same behind: Take B across, then G across

❖ Make about 55mm of eight-strand square sennit, apply a temporary seizing and make an eight-strand diamond knot. Follow it round to double it.

❖ Then follows 55mm of alternate 4+4 crown sennit (similar to the 3+3 on page 31 but a little harder to get to sit well), an eight-strand star knot (similar to the six-strand on page 35), then 60mm of four-strand crown sennit with pairs.

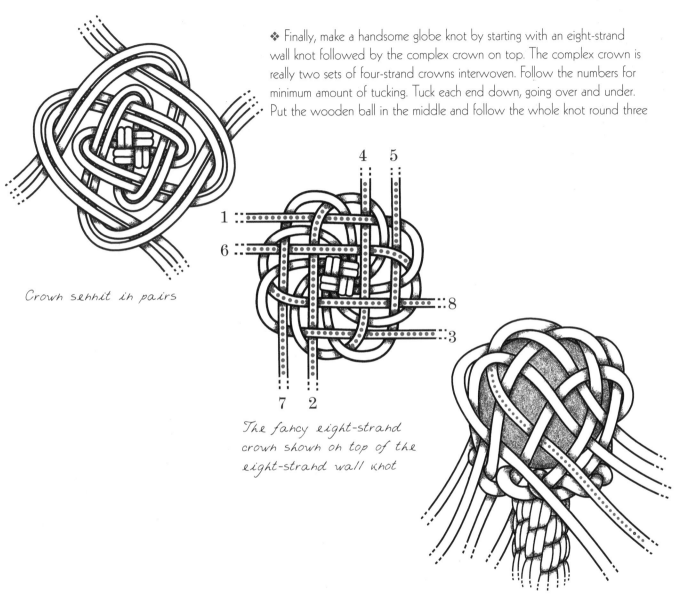

❖ Finally, make a handsome globe knot by starting with an eight-strand wall knot followed by the complex crown on top. The complex crown is really two sets of four-strand crowns interwoven. Follow the numbers for minimum amount of tucking. Tuck each end down, going over and under. Put the wooden ball in the middle and follow the whole knot round three

Crown sennit in pairs

4   5
1
6
8
3
7   2

The fancy eight-strand crown shown on top of the eight-strand wall knot

❖ This globe knot takes a minimum of 550mm of line, so make sure that the shortest of your eight strands is at least this long before you start. If you wish, add extra coloured Turk's heads at any place on the bell rope.

Extra tucks with all strands after the fancy eight-strand crown on top of eight-strand wall makes the globe knot

TRICOLOUR *bell rope*

 *I spotted a tricolour bell rope in a Rotterdam ship's chandlers. It was made up in layers just as the Dutch flag, red at the top, white in the middle and blue at the bottom. This set me thinking how the unknown tyer had achieved this clear division of colour. I then realised that, at each colour break, there was a diamond knot; hidden behind the diamond knot was the change of colour.*

I do not recall exactly which kind of sennit was used to build up the body of the piece, but the solution here with six strands crowned in pairs will work just as well with eight strands worked in pairs. In many ways this is related to the way in which the pyramid key ring grew (see page 32), only there is a swap of colour rather than a growing of size.

I finished the end with a six-strand globe knot based on the fancy crown on page 46, but you could easily finish with a star knot. While I speak of this being a tricoloured bell rope, the same method could make you a two-coloured item or, for that matter, you could go mad and make it a longer, many-coloured bell rope. Why not try the same colour change with a lanyard or dog lead?

MATERIALS

* 3 x 1m of 3mm cord, colour one

* 3 x 1m of 3mm cord, colour two

* 3 x 1.5m of 3mm cord, colour three

KNOTS USED

* Three-strand sennit - see page 163

* Temporary seizing, probably a constrictor knot - see page 12

* Three-strand diamond knot tied in pairs - see page 112 - or a Matthew Walker in six strands - see page 81

* Crown sennit in pairs - see page 39

* Wall and crown somewhat like the manrope knot but tied with six ends - see page 79

* Star knot finish - see page 35 - or six-strand sphere covering based on the six-strand fancy crown - see page 47

METHOD

❖ Start the bell rope in a similar manner to either the deluxe key ring on page 29 or the bell rope worked with six ends on page 34. With the six ends as three pairs, make 50mm of three-strand crown sennit. Under the last crown lock in three more lengths of line of a different colour, as shown below.

The introduction of new coloured lines

❖ Treating these new pieces as three pairs, make another 50mm of three-strand crown sennit, leaving the six original coloured ends free.

❖ With these six original coloured ends, make a diamond knot by first making a crown knot and then a wall knot below, double the knot, tighten and trim the ends. This knot should just disguise the changeover of colours.

❖ You can now introduce a third colour in exactly the same way and perhaps make another 50–60mm, the join again being covered with a diamond in the second colour.

❖ Finish your bell rope with either a six-strand star knot or a six-strand sphere covering based on the six-strand fancy crown on page 46.

Simple SIDE FENDER

'Any piece of cable that is cut off, most commonly any part of an old cable, is called a junk. Such as this they hang for fenders by the ships' sides.'

So wrote Sir Henry Mainwaring in 1623 in his Seaman's Dictionary, *the earliest nautical dictionary in English. Today it is still a good way to make a beefy side fender for a barge or tug. I have made them using old ship's mooring cables and offcuts of heavy coir from wrap-round fenders. The cable may be just stitched together with some line, but I prefer either to make a proper seizing or even better, if I have the time, to make two or three Turk's heads round the cables, thereby giving these simplest of fenders that proper seaman's look. I think that three or four hanging over the side can really look quite smart and not cost a great deal.*

If you use your imagination, the same idea can be developed to make a fender with lanyard at each end so that it can be hung lengthways to protect the leeboard on a barge.

LOCK ➡

Jolly Zephyr

For this type of fender you can use whatever rope is to hand, but here are the requirements for a couple of basic variations.

Variation 1:

✳ 2 x 2m of 60mm square plait old ship's mooring cable

✳ 3 x 8m of 12mm polypropylene for the seizings

✳ 1 x 3m of 14mm polypropylene for the lanyard

Variation 2:

✳ 1 x 2m of 96mm (actual diameter) coir

✳ 3 x 7.5m of 14mm manila for the Turk's head

✳ 1 x 3m of 14mm manila for the lanyard

KNOTS USED

✳ Constrictor knot - see page 12

✳ Flat seizing or three-lead, five-bight Turk's head - see page 44

METHOD
Variation 1

❖ Fold both pieces of the heavy cable in half, making the bend as tight as possible by giving it a good beating with a heavy mallet. If you are using very heavy coir you will find that it is much harder to bend than ship's cable; you may well have to resort to a Spanish windlass or, ideally, that rarest of beasts, the rigger's screw.

❖ If you are using two pieces of cable put the two pieces together with the bends at the same end. Hold the folded rope or ropes in place with a couple of turns of a temporary binding of some sort. My favourite is a constrictor knot, as you can pull the ends and the whole thing cranks up nice and tight.

❖ Now put on the permanent seizing of seven or eight turns. I start with either a constrictor knot round all strands or, for very heavy rope, a constrictor round one strand. Pull very tight on each turn; finish off with a couple of frapping turns and lock in place as shown below.

Flat seizing

Variation 2

❖ Alternatively, a three-lead, five-bight Turk's head, followed round three times, will serve a similar purpose and look even more handsome. It will help to practise tying the Turk's head round your fingers first. You can use your thumb to hold the turns in place. You are making a three-strand continuous plait or sennit.

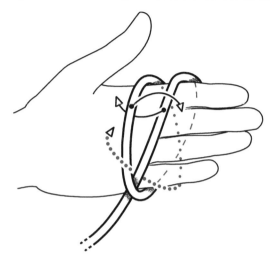

Start of the three-lead, five-bight Turk's head

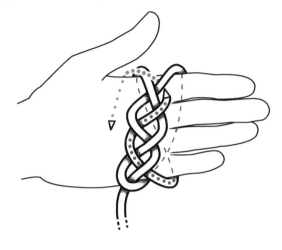

Stage two of the three-lead, five-bight Turk's head

❖ When all the seizings or Turk's heads are in place, trim the bottom; you will need to sharpen your knife a few times to get through this heavy rope. I use a very coarse stone with water as a lubricant to sharpen my favourite knife. For the very heaviest of ship's cable I sometimes even resort to a hacksaw to get through the rope.

❖ After the end has been trimmed, all that remains is for the lanyard to be fitted with a splice through the top loop, whip or back splice the inboard end of the lanyard, and hang over the side to protect your craft.

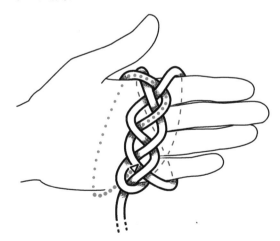

Beginning of doubling the three-lead, five-bight Turk's head

Side fender using the CROWN SENNIT

👉 *There are many ways of making a side fender, all using the crown sennit, put together in various ways. This is the way I usually do it.*

On board ship, worn-out old rope would have been used, whereas shore-based fender makers would have used new material, certainly on the outside. Coir has always been one of the preferred materials for salt-water craft, as it is light (it floats), fairly resistant to rot in salt water and, for its size, not expensive.

If you are making the fender for yourself you can use any old rope that you can get your hands on. Leonard Popple in his book Advanced Ropework *recommends making a miniature before commencing a full-size fender. This allows you to see how it all goes together and saves the waste of rope. You could always make a giant key ring out of your miniature.*

Sometimes people get a little confused between the crown knot and the wall knot (see page 46). One is the upside down version of the other, so it rather depends on how you look at it when you are making the knots. I start work with the top of the fender between my knees and work upwards, so this is the view from which I name the knots.

The Swedish fid with its hollow allows the final splicing back to be done both neatly and speedily (I find that a little dab of tallow on the spike dramatically eases the amount of push required).

I have given the amounts of materials needed for a range of sizes. Much bigger fenders can be made by starting with two lengths of rope, giving twelve strands. A bigger core will, of course, be needed, and the end crown can be made with pairs of strands.

MATERIALS

* ✱ 3-4m of tarred marline or similar to make the seizing at the start

* ✱ 200mm long x 100mm diameter fender: 2m of 24mm coir (no core)

* ✱ 250mm long x 100mm diameter fender: 2.5m of 24mm coir (no core)

* ✱ 250mm long x 125mm diameter fender: 2.7m of 28mm coir (plus scrap for core)

* ✱ 350mm long x 125mm diameter fender: 4m of 28mm coir (plus scrap for core)

* ✱ Note that coir rope tends to be bigger than its stated size, so if you are using other materials they need to be a little bigger than above. Alternatively, make the core a little bigger, or be content with a slightly smaller fender.

KNOTS USED

* ✱ Flat seizing - see page 43
* ✱ Six-strand wall knot
* ✱ Six-strand crown knot
* ✱ Special six strand crown
* ✱ Splicing

METHOD

For a 200mm x 100mm fender:

❖ It is a good idea to make a fender without a core to start with; it gives you one less thing to worry about. Fold the rope in half and put a flat seizing round the bight, to make the eye at the top of the fender. Put either tape or a temporary whipping on each of the six rope strand ends and unlay the rope, giving six strands to work with.

❖ Make a six-strand wall knot with these ends as shown below; this gives the fender a sort of shoulder.

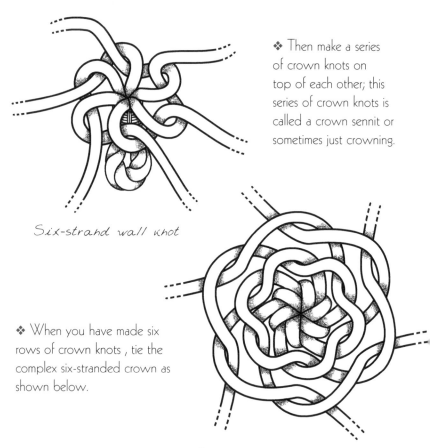

Six-strand wall knot

❖ Then make a series of crown knots on top of each other; this series of crown knots is called a crown sennit or sometimes just crowning.

❖ When you have made six rows of crown knots, tie the complex six-stranded crown as shown below.

Six-strand crown sennit

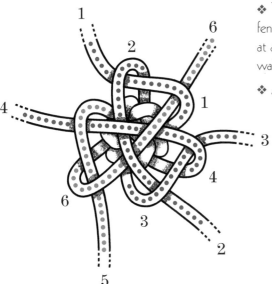

1   6

2

4   1

   3

  6   4

     3

      2

5

The fancy six-strand crown - please follow the colours for a minimum of tucking

❖ Turn the fender round and splice the strands back up the outside of the fender to the shoulder. (I find it best to make one complete row of tucks at a time.) When the shoulder has been reached, tuck the ends under the wall knot and out right next to the seizing, as shown below.

❖ All strands need to be spliced back as shown.

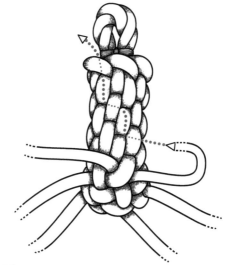

Trim the ends and roll under the foot to shape

∼ VARIATION: BIGGER FENDERS WITH CORE ∼

For bigger sizes, use a core made up from either six or seven rope strands from the same size rope that you are using for the fender. Once you get going, you can use the offcuts from previous fenders. The core is pushed into the hole in the centre of the first crown knot and held in place by the subsequent rows of crowning. Trim before making the complex crown at the end. Splice on a lanyard and hang over the side of your vessel.

Make:
- Eight rows of crowns for the 250mm x 100mm fender
- Six rows of crowns for the 250mm x 125mm fender
- Ten rows of crowns for the 350mm x 125mm fender

HITCHING *over a plastic fender*

Most rope fenders consist of a core of some kind and a needle-hitched cover. Needle hitching or half hitching, as it is sometimes called, is a very versatile covering technique. It can be done using almost any size of material from 1mm up to 24mm diameter. It is found all over the world covering all sorts of things from tassel heads to clay pots, fenders and knife handles.

It has one disadvantage in that it is rather time-consuming. So when you start using this technique don't be disappointed at your rate of progress; it does need time and patience. It can take about an hour to use up about 10m of 10mm or 12mm line. Be warned, it can be rather addictive; there is a tendency to 'just do a bit more'.

Covering a small sausage-shaped plastic fender is a good way to learn the technique, and it's a good way to finish up with a traditional looking fender without the extra time and trouble of making up the core.

You could, of course, make up a bundle of old rope with a loop at one or both ends and cover that in exactly the same way. Building up on a plastic fender base is a good idea for larger fenders, as the core will be nearly all air and the finished fender a lot lighter than if a bundle of old rope had been used.

MATERIALS

The hitching of the cover depends so much on the size of the rope and the size of the fender, and on how tight and close the hitches are, that it is only possible to give a very rough guide of the quantity of rope needed. I reckon that about 160m of 10mm or 12mm rope will give about a square metre of cover. If you can keep track of the material you use you will get a closer picture for yourself, but you will still have surprises. It always seems to take more material and more time than I estimate!

* This means that, to cover a 400mm x 125mm diameter sausage-shaped fender, you need about 24-26m of 10mm three-strand rope.

* A 600mm x 200mm diameter sausage fender needs about 55-60m of 10mm three-strand rope.

* This can either be a natural material such as sisal, manila or hemp, or a synthetic, but try not to have a too hard-laid (stiff) rope as this makes it more difficult to get the hitches to pull tight and bed down.

* It is possible to use braided rope or the strand from a bigger rope, but you are then restricted in your method of joining in new ends.

KNOTS USED

* Half hitch

* Long splice if you prefer to make a spliced join in the rope - see method

METHOD

❖ Cut 20m of line and tape the ends into 100mm long points.

❖ Put the rope round the middle of the fender, and adjust to give two equal ends of 10m. A 10m length is probably the most efficient length; if shorter there are too many joins and a longer length takes forever to pull through.

❖ Start hitching from the centre, putting the first row of about fourteen hitches for the 125mm diameter fender or about twenty-two hitches for the 200mm diameter fender. Space these evenly round one side, then pull the other end tight before locking everything in place by hitching round the second side.

❖ Carry on hitching out from the middle, trying to keep the starting point from slipping away from the centre of the fender.

❖ When the two sides have used up almost all the rope, assess how much of the fender has been covered and therefore how much more rope will be needed to cover the rest of that side, and make a note of what you think you will need.

❖ This new rope will need to be joined in. This can be done in a couple of ways, either with a long splice, leaving the tails to be trimmed off later, or by bringing the new rope from under a couple of the previous rows and out of the hitch in place of the old short end which can then be covered by subsequent rows. Carry on hitching to the end. As the fender tapers away it's possible to shape the cover by dropping every second or third hitch, finally burying the end back under a couple of rows of hitching.

❖ By seeing how much line was used on the first end you may be able to have a slightly shorter end on the second half, but do not cut too short or you may need to join in yet another short end.

❖ If you want to cover a teardrop-shaped fender, it is possible to start at the narrow end and gradually increase the number of hitches by making two hitches in a space instead of the usual single hitch.

Starting, hitching both ways and increasing/reducing hitches

Bow *fender*

☞ *The scale of the bow fender can vary enormously. Whatever the scale, the basic method of construction is the same; there are two basic components: the core and the cover. The core takes all the punishment and, in many ways, it is the fender. The cover is there to protect the core and should look good.*

Much of the beauty of a bow fender depends on its shape (that is, the shape of the core), so it is essential to take plenty of care when building this up. There should be no lumps or bumps. It can help to finish with a layer of sacking to give a smooth base over which the hitching will go. The two side pieces, or 'legs', should be symmetrical.

At the heart of the core is a 'backbone' rope or chain. For all but the smallest fenders I prefer a chain, but some people use a heavy wire rope and for a light job a backbone of rope will be fine. If you do use rope, use a synthetic material that will not rot before the fender cover has worn out.

Fitted to the backbone can be one, two or more short tails that will help to hold the fender up at the bow. It is always disappointing to see a bow fender drooping down; I like to see it tight up and square, but occasionally this has to be sacrificed when the fender is needed lower down the stem and there are no appropriate fittings to make the legs fast to.

Half hitching (see page 50) is the most versatile method to cover the core. The size of the rope used for this will vary but should be in proportion to the finished fender; 6mm may be fine for a delicate job for a skiff, 12mm or 14mm for a work boat of 10–15m length, and 20–24mm for the largest tug fender.

The type of rope used depends on taste and material available: three-strand rope means that you may long-splice lengths together and it can be either natural or synthetic fibre. Natural fibre rope such as manila or sisal, or even hemp, is likely to rot after a few years, especially if the fender is left on all year round.

This decay can be slowed down by painting or dunking the fender from time to time in some form of preservative; be it clear Cuprinol, creosote, thinned down tar or even old sump oil! It rather depends on how you want the fender to look and how happy you will be to make another one.

Polypropylene is a low-cost synthetic rope that many people use. I quite like the staple-spun polypropylene (the slightly hairy-looking one), which is a fair compromise in the cost/look/ life stakes. I have seen some handsome fenders in black polypropylene.

There are a number of synthetic hemp lookalikes, which give a near-traditional look, but it is worth checking how resistant they are to UV breakdown, as some are better than others. Nylon or polyester will last the longest, but they are often hard-laid, which makes hitching hard work. They are also the most expensive and do have a tendency to look a little modern.

A lot of rope is needed and it will take you a lot of time to hitch the cover, but on the other hand I hope you will get pleasure from making the fender.

With all the work of hitching the cover of the fender, you may wish to add a Turk's head at the centre to protect the hitching at this vulnerable point. It is easier to replace than having to remake part of the cover, and it certainly gives the fender additional style!

MATERIALS

For the backbone of a fender between 1-2m overall:

✱ A piece of 6mm or 8mm short- or long-link galvanised chain

✱ One or two shackles and short pieces of chain (optional) for central suspension points

For the core:

✱ It is sensible to use old scrap rope, in all sizes from 6mm to 50mm, if you can get hold of it. I prefer to use synthetic rope, as it doesn't hold the water as much, and preferably polypropylene, which is the lightest of the synthetics. It is useful to have all sizes available, and you will use a surprisingly large amount.

For hitching of the cover:

✱ Lengths of rope based on the guide figures for covering a plastic fender (160m of 10-12mm rope for 1m²)

For a Turk's head rubbing piece:

✱ Rope of the same or a larger diameter than you used to hitch the cover

✱ A four-lead, five-bight Turk's head (see page 89), followed round three times, will need approximately 18-20 times the circumference of the fender.

KNOTS USED

✱ Constrictor knot - see page 12

✱ Packer's knot - see page 12

✱ Half hitch - see page 50

✱ Four-lead, five-bight Turk's head - see page 89

METHOD

❖ Measure the chain to be used, not forgetting that it will be in the centre of the fender so it will need to be longer than the inner part of the fender, and allow an extra 150mm each end for tails outside the fender. Mark the middle of the chain.

❖ Rig the chain backbone tight between two swivels at about waist height. If there is a need for suspension chains fit them now with a shackle either at the centre, if just one, or a few inches either side of the centre if you use two suspension chains. A really long fender may have four or even six suspension chains. Occasionally there is also a call for a chain to hold the fender in place down below the fender.

❖ With the suspension chains rigged, fit four thin ropes in the space formed by the interlinking of the chain links. Tie these ropes in place using either a series of constrictor knots or one of the variations of packer's knots. If you have it available, wrap round the four ropes and chain with more thin rope, starting at the middle and working out, being sure to treat both sides equally.

❖ Unless the fender is to finish up almost straight, remove the wrapped chain from between the swivels and bend it to the approximate curve of the finished fender.

❖ Put one long heavy rope to the front of the chain, probably going almost the entire length of the backbone. Put shorter pieces above, below and behind the backbone to build up the shape of fender you are aiming at. There will always be a little flexibility, but the nearer the correct shape the better. Tie these tightly to the backbone.

❖ It is then worth tapering the ends so that there are not too many steps where each rope ends. Add extra rope as required to get the shape and size (thinner ropes give a smoother shape), stagger the ends and keep the shape symmetrical.

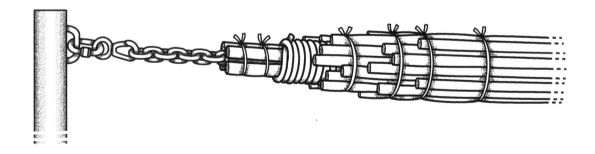

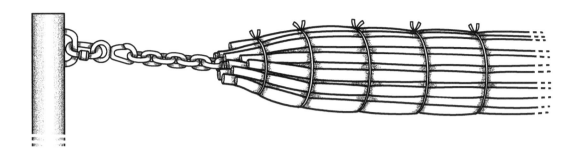

Building the core of the fender, shown straight, but could be bent to shape for the later stages if required

❖ The finished core needs to be about 100–150mm less in circumference than the finished fender size. It is important to get the size and shape right before putting on its jacket.

❖ When you are satisfied with the form and shape of the fender, I find that it helps to cover the whole thing with sacking of some sort, to give a smooth final finish to hitch over. I use hessian, jute, burlap or sisal sacking if the cover is to be natural, and the woven white or cream polypropylene sacking if the cover is to be a synthetic rope. Ideally the colour of sacking is somewhere near the colour of the rope to be used.

❖ This cover is best sewn in place using a packing needle, working out from the middle and getting the cover tight over the core. Some people prefer to wrap the whole fender core with adhesive tape.

❖ You are now ready to cover the core. You can start in the middle and work to the ends, which is fine if the fender is almost straight, but if it is curved I find it best to start at each end and work to the middle. I actually suspend the fender from the leg end, then it is easy to work round and round adding hitches as the fender grows in diameter by putting two hitches side by side into the space of one hitch rather than the usual one.

❖ To aid symmetry, work a length of rope on one leg, then change and work on the other. When both sides meet at the centre there will be a gap. Hitch round the gap in a circle dropping hitches as needed until it is completely filled in.

❖ When you have finished hitching the cover (well done!), you could add a Turk's head in heavier rope round the middle as extra chafe protection. I favour a four-lead five-bight Turk's head as I feel it will sit evenly either side of the bow, but a three-lead version will do almost as well. I have worked to the original 1930s specification for a tug fender that had five Turk's heads round it at various points; it certainly looked very handsome when it was finished.

Ring *fender*

For hundreds of years fenders have been made from rope. One simple but handsome type is the ring fender, sometimes known as a donut fender. Such ring fenders were illustrated as long ago as 1829 by EW Cooke hanging over the side of a couple of Thames peter boats. They can occasionally be seen today hanging over the stern quarter of a motor 'Butty'-style canal boat, and they are occasionally still made in the Royal Navy.

This fender can be made in various sizes: from 150mm outside, 50mm centre for a small skiff, to 250–300mm outside diameter for a canal boat, and right up to 900mm outside for something much bigger.

Coir was always the preferred rope, but I have used cotton for small sizes and old rope could be used if appropriate.

Those of you with a more modern frame of mind will realise that an old tyre with suitable drainage holes will be much improved in looks if it is covered with ringbolt hitching. It can help to wrap the tyre in sacking to help disguise the black rubber. A very good modern-day ring fender.

MATERIALS

✱ Small stuff for temporary seizings

✱ To work out how much you need, make up a short dummy section round your base ring or tyre; use just single hitches tight together and then use that short section to work out how much is needed to cover the entire ring, and add a bit for luck, as it is better too long than too short.

✱ If you wish to use the three-strand ringbolt hitching, divide your estimated length into two-thirds and one-third.

✱ As a very rough guide, the 150mm fender takes about 4m of 10mm for the core and 6m of 5mm for the outer hitching, while the 900mm fender uses 23m of 32mm coir for the core and about 36m of 20mm for the outer hitching.

✱ Car tyres are best covered with 12mm or 14mm rope, using something like 50m, but check as mentioned above.

KNOTS USED

✱ Packer's knot - see page 12

✱ Marlinespike hitch - see page 13

✱ Ringbolt hitching with a single strand or ringbolt hitching three-strand

✱ Eye splice for the lanyard - see page 71

METHOD

❖ First the base is built. Lay a few lengths of light line which will be used as seizings later, put a paint tin the size of the required centre hole on top of these and build up a coil of rope, or cheese (the proper name for such a coil is a cheese!). Pull each row of rope firmly as it is coiled. When you have the right size of 'donut', remove the tin and tie up with a packer's knot, giving a good pull using the marlinespike hitch.

❖ When the ring is firmly seized into shape, it can then be covered using ringbolt hitching. The simplest method is just a series of half hitches, made in alternate directions with a single strand.

❖ A much finer job can be made using three strands, the hitches being made in turn. This time, divide the rope to be used into two-thirds and one-third. Start with a constrictor knot tied in the middle of the longer piece round the core holding the shorter piece in place and start your hitching with the shorter piece.

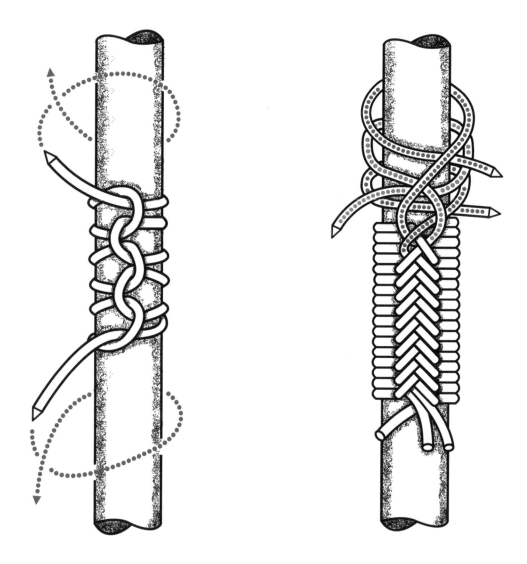

Cover using a series of half hitches, left, or three strands, right

❖ To finish, whichever covering you use, tuck the ends under a few of the starting turns. The fender now needs its lanyard spliced on and it is ready to be slung over the side.

RNLI-*style* BOW PUDDING

☞ *The UK's Royal National Lifeboat Institute (RNLI) lifeboats have until very recently sported a particular style of fender called 'bow pudding'. This style of fender is exactly the same as the pudding illustrated in D'Arcy Lever's* Young Sea Officer's Sheet Anchor, *first published in 1808.*

Shortly after the RNLI workshops stopped making these fenders, I was asked to make one for their RIB tender that serviced the Spurn Point lifeboat. I asked what was going to happen to the old one and they said it would go in the rubbish skip. I protested and suggested they send it to me as a pattern; so I now have what is probably the last pudding made in their workshops.

While I knew what the fender looked like (indeed, I had a number of photographs of men making them) and was sure that I could replicate its look, I did not know the 'trade secrets' to making a true bow pudding. Luckily

LUCY LAVERS

59

a couple of years before I had a brief correspondence with one of the men, Frank 'Winkle' Ide, who had worked in the RNLI workshops at Poole. Luck was on my side as I was able to find his phone number and a phone conversation with him set me right. So with that stroke of fortune, the special secrets have been preserved and I can share them with you.

The fender consists of a core built up in exactly the same way as the bow fender on page 53, although the RNLI use a rope or wire backbone with a thimble each end as a hard eye, rather than the chain I prefer. The cover is woven using an even number of what they call 'nettles' running the length of the fender as 'warps', with a lighter line being wrapped round the body as a 'weft'. It is the tightening of the weft that is the very special secret.

MATERIALS

As there are many different sizes of pudding, here are some guidelines for the cover for two sizes. The exact number of nettles needed does rather depend on the exact size of the rope used; remember they should be an even number.

* A pudding 1.4m long, with 450mm mid girth and 190mm end girth, uses about 72-84 nettles of 6mm rope, 3m long.

* A pudding 1.8m long, with 900mm mid girth and 250mm end girth, uses about 110 nettles of 6mm rope, 4m long.

* For the wrapping you will need plenty of line about 4mm in diameter: at least 80m for the smaller pudding, but have more to join on if needed.

* The core uses scrap built up round a backbone of 18mm rope.

KNOTS USED

* Constrictor knot - see page 12 - or packer's knot - see page 12
* Special double tuck tightening turns
* Crown and tuck finish

METHOD

❖ The RNLI pudding is made up laid straight and flat on the bench.

❖ Start by making an eye splice each end of the backbone, with a thimble if you wish. Build up the core of the fender as described on page 47. The size of the core needs to be about 75mm less in circumference than the desired finished fender.

❖ For the last layer of the core I try to use rope of a similar type to that being used for the cover so nothing is obvious if there is a slight gap in the cover.

❖ Cut a good number of pieces of 6mm line for the nettles. I find it helps to tape at the measured mark and cut through the tape so that you get two ends taped at one go.

❖ Lay the nettles along the length of the fender, holding them in place at the middle with a temporary tie, using either a packer's knot or a constrictor knot, according to your taste. The nettles should be touching one another at the middle.

❖ Add additional nettles as needed to completely cover the middle part of the fender. Make sure that you have an even number.

❖ Take one side of the temporary seizing and pull each alternate nettle back towards the other end. Middle the line you will use for wrapping and, starting at the outer ends, make up each end into a hank. Pass right round the whole body of the fender, on top of the lower set of nettles laying along the body of the fender and tuck twice, making the double tucked binding shown below; give a good pull, using a marlinespike hitch in the line to get maximum heave.

❖ Make a second pass, repeat the double tuck binding and give another good heave; note how the second pass when pulled still tightens the first pass a little more. It is this special way of tightening the 'weft' that gives rise to the puzzle that there appear to be two passes in some places and three in others.

❖ Now swap over the nettles, pulling the tied down ones back hard against the binding and replacing them with the other set; repeat your series of two double tuck tightening turns. Take care to arrange the start of these tightening turns to give no sign of the swap-over of nettles. You should now be able to see that you are starting to create a woven cover.

❖ Carry on like this for a few more rows before turning the fender round and taking out the temporary seizing. Using the other end of line, repeat in a similar manner to the other side. Try to keep everything symmetric.

❖ As the fender starts to taper, you will need to leave out some of the warp nettles, perhaps two sets per row. I tie two from the top and one from the bottom layer together so that I can see that I am dropping in a systematic manner, evenly round the body of the fender. When you come to make the next pass you will leave two of the three under the now slightly smaller cover; it will be apparent as to which you leave to give you a neat woven look. Leave these dropped ends under the cover tied together and temporarily seized near the end eye of the backbone to be dealt with later.

❖ To keep symmetry I do the same number of passes each side, perhaps checking with a tape measure from time to time that all is well. Keep on dropping cover nettles as needed until you reach each end of the core.

❖ For the final row, leave the bottom layer of nettles in place, bring down the top layer of nettles and then make three double-tucked bindings, holding all down tightly, before the final finish of crown and tucks are made, as shown below.

❖ Firstly crown the top layer by tucking each end under its neighbour, then tuck back three tucks under the adjacent top nettle, pulling all good and tight. When you have completed all tucks, trim the ends, but not too close or they may well pop out when fitting the pudding.

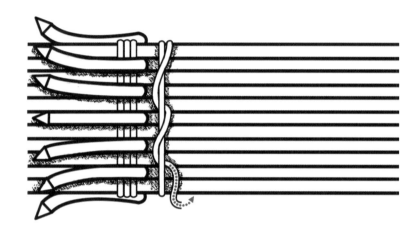

❖ Traditionally the RNLI bow pudding has always been made straight and then bent round the bow for fitting. However, this always causes bulges on the inner part of the curve. To reduce this (it is not possible to completely eliminate them), before making the finishing crowning and tucking, bend the fender round a post or such, perhaps using a block and tackle made fast to each end eye to give extra purchase. You could even resort to some form of Spanish windlass, tightening a line joining the two end eyes.

❖ Having bent the fender, pull hard on all of the nettles on the inner curve of the fender using a marlinespike hitch to give some grip. Work systematically, so none is missed. By thus tightening the inner nettles, including those nettles you dropped in the shaping, you will reduce the bulges to a great degree. This shaping does make the finishing a little harder, as you are now dealing with a banana-shaped bow pudding. It is up to you which way you choose to finish your pudding.

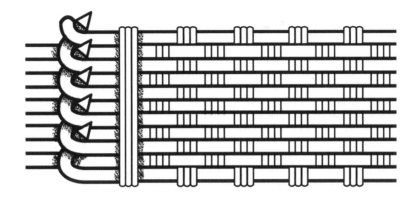

Finishing with the double tuck binding and the
top layer crowned

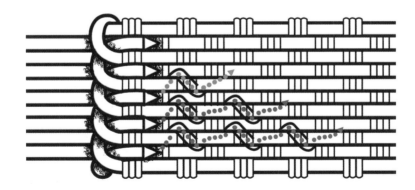

Tuck the crowned ends back 3 times to finish

Button FENDER

☞ *The narrowboats found on British canals have developed their own special pieces of ropework. Working in and out of so many locks the fenders evolved into a distinct style and shape. On the bow is usually a button fender about 300mm in diameter and 200mm deep, usually with a hitched cover. This fender is used to push open the lock gates gently.*

On the stern of the motor 'Butty', there can be a long, fat sausage-shaped fender, about 600–700mm long and 250mm in diameter at the centre, tapering off each side; this is called a tip cat and protects the rudder that sticks out behind the main hull. If one tip cat is not enough there can be a second tip cat or another button; there can even be two tip cats and a button, a very handsome arrangement when fitted properly with just a little upward tilt. Some boaters prefer to have a single button, which may be a little longer (300mm) than that used at the bow.

Side fenders tend to be rather on the long and thin side (175mm in diameter, 300–400mm long) because in many of the canals there is very little room between the boat and the side of the lock or tunnel wall.

As with all fenders, it is very important to make up a good, solid, well-shaped core. The tip cat is constructed very much like the bow fender already described. The button requires a different approach to the building of its core to ensure that it is solid and stable enough to withstand the hard treatment it will receive.

When the button fender is first fitted, it's a good idea to find a quiet spot to very gently push square up against something, to bed the fender in place before it is used in anger!

MATERIALS

For a button fender 300mm in diameter and 200mm deep:

✱ *Scrap rope for the core, preferably synthetic*

✱ *1 x 1200mm of 6mm chain or with a second 1200mm piece doubled and joined to the middle of the first chain to give two top chains*

✱ *32m of 12mm rope for the cover (natural or synthetic, as you wish)*

KNOTS USED

✱ *Packer's knot - see page 12*

✱ *Hitching - see page 49*

✱ *Long splice (if this is your preferred method of joining extra line when hitching) - see page 96*

METHOD

❖ The core is basically just a solid coil of old rope, 230mm in diameter by 180mm high, tied nice and tight. The problem is how to make and tie your coil good and tight. I use a method explained to me by Ike Argent, an old boater who was greatly respected for his well-made fenders.

❖ A thin metal pipe of about 25mm diameter is held upright in a vice (a workmate-type bench works very well), sticking up through a disc of wood a little over the maximum diameter of the base you want to make. It helps if the disc is marked with a number of concentric circles. Drop three or four pieces of synthetic cord of about 3mm diameter down the middle of the pipe, bring their other ends down the side of the pipe and lay them out evenly round the base with their ends hanging down the sides of the disc.

❖ Start wrapping the core material round the pipe, keeping the thin lines in place. If your core material is all the same diameter you can build up your coil in a series of flat discs, working out to the required size (230mm) and then back in again.

❖ When the disc is about half the height of the fender, place the chain or chains in the middle and carry on up to the top of the button fender base (180mm). If you are using a variety of material to build up your core, you can wrap it round the pipe to the height required (180mm) and work back down again to the base. This way you will have to put the chain in the middle and wrap up and down round it until you reach the 230mm diameter wanted.

Note that the ties go down the centre of the pipe

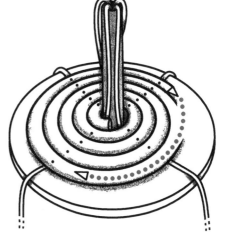

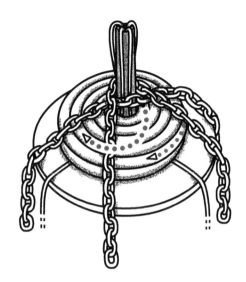

Coiling up the core and putting in the chains

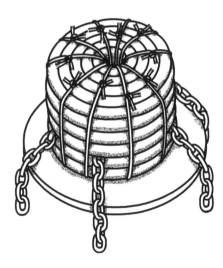

The core all finished and tied up

❖ When the core is the right size, pull out the cord ends that are down inside the pipe and tie each end to its own other end with a packer's knot, giving a good heave tight as you do.

❖ Remove the pipe, bed the rope down with a few blows from a mallet and apply extra bindings to ensure the core will hold together come what may. You may wish to cover this base with some sacking, it certainly helps to hitch over a smooth-surfaced core.

❖ Put the middle of the cover rope round the middle of the fender core and start hitching out each side.

❖ When you reach the edge of the core, decrease by skipping every third hitch for a whole row. Then make a full row, skipping every fourth hitch, and finally skip every other hitch until you reach the centre and finish by burying the end, bringing it right out to the edge.

❖ Give the fender another good beating with a mallet before finishing the other side in the same manner.

❖ All that remains is to fit the fender good and tight to the boat. It is a good idea to saw through one of the links of the chain so that, should a fender get caught in a lock, the chain gives way before the boat ends up under the water.

Rope LADDERS

There are lots of styles of rope ladder. Some ladders are made entirely of rope, some have a round wooden rung and some, like the heavy pilot ladder, are made with flat steps held in place with chocks and long spreader steps to stop the ladder twisting. Most of these ladders require a lot of work with a great deal of seizing in of the wooden ladder rungs.

A few of the simpler ways to make a rope ladder include using a series of marlinespike hitches (see page 13) round a wooden bar, making very sure that you get the pull direction right. Frankly, I would not recommend this, as the bar could still slip out sideways (there is a simple knotted all-rope ladder for very occasional use that will do in an emergency).

The other method involves using a round wooden rung and square or eight-plait rope, also known as anchor plait, that makes a much better and more permanent job.

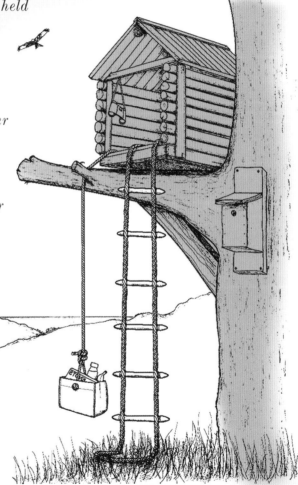

MATERIALS

The length of rope required depends on the length of ladder you are making. You need to allow extra for rope at the top and any long tails at the bottom of the ladder.

For the all-rope ladder:

✱ 1.3m of 12mm or 14mm rope per rung (including the rope both sides between it and the next rung)

For the ladder using square plait:

✱ 700mm of 14 or 16mm per rung (including the rope both sides between it and the next rung)

✱ The required number of round wooden rungs made from a hard wood, ideally ash (usually 300-400mm long with 25mm diameter for the shorter and 32mm diameter for the longer version)

KNOTS USED

All-rope ladder:

✱ 'Boas bowline' (a variation on the bowline)- see diagram (A)

✱ A form of the sheet bend - see diagram (B)

✱ Square-plait rope ladder:

✱ Uses the structure of the rope to hold the rung in place

METHOD

❖ For the all-rope ladder, middle the rope and on one side tie the Boas bowline, as shown below; the loop forms the first rung of the ladder. With the other side, tuck the rope as shown to make a sheet bend, adjusting the 'rung' so that it is level. Reverse the arrangement between rungs to get a balanced set of knots. Rungs need to be no more than 300mm apart.

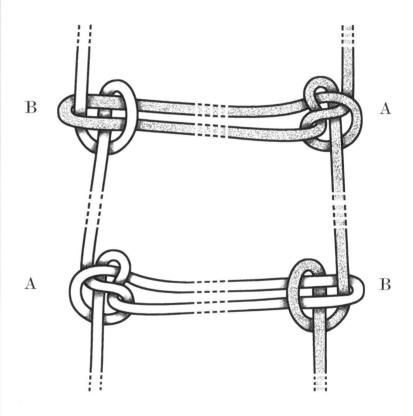

B   A

A   B

Make knot (A), the Boas bowline, before making the sheet bend (B)

❖ Using the square plait, it is a matter of working the ladder rung between the plait, to give four strands either side of the groove in the rung. This is not so simple and will be a tight fit. The rope will tighten up as soon as any strain is put on it and so hold the rung in place.

❖ To ease the rung into the rope, first open up a bit of a hole and then use a pilot spike with an open tube end the size of the rung, or if you are getting your rungs turned for you, it helps to have a short-tapered outer end or one with an acorn-shaped point.

❖ Again, space the rungs about 300mm apart. I find it best to stretch the rope doubled between two fixed points, to give the two sides. Put in the first rung both sides, and then count down the same number of parts of plait each side, keeping all twist out of the rope, and put your next rung in.

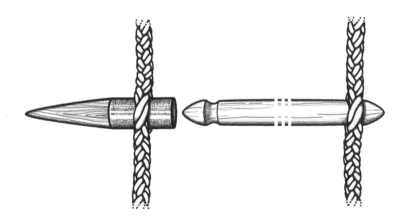

Use a pilot spike to insert the wooden rungs

SIMPLE *lanyard*

A tool dropped when working aloft is bad news – at best a damaged deck, at worst serious injury to a fellow crew member. If it falls over the side it's gone forever and at sea there is no local chandler's to take more of your hard-earned cash for a replacement. The best and safest thing to do is to keep your tools on a lead, then they cannot run away. Fit them with a lanyard!

Here is a simple lanyard with just a little decorative detail, that goes round the neck and allows the knife or other tool to slip into a pocket or sheath. Make the lanyard long enough so that you can stretch your arm out fully, with a loop that will fit easily over your head.

It is possible to make the knots sliding so as to adjust the loop, but a sliding knot on this kind of lanyard is not a good idea. In fact, it is a better idea to have a weak link between tool and lanyard, as it is no good saving your tool at the expense of strangling yourself.

Made a little longer and adjustable, if you wish, the whole lanyard can go right round the waist with a clasp knife on its end that slips neatly into a pocket.

The same style of lanyard, perhaps with a whistle on its end, can go round the shoulder and into the breast pocket of a uniform. By using heavier rope, say 10mm with a clip fixed to the smaller loop and making the other loop just big enough to put your hand through, you will have a dog lead, or is it a dog lanyard?

METHOD

❖ Put a temporary seizing about 200mm from the end of the rope, then unlay the three strands, taping the ends so that they do not come undone. Form a loop of about 70mm and tuck the three strands as in the start of an eye splice, which is shown below.

Eye splice start

❖ Now make a crown knot round the rope, followed by a wall beneath the crown, thus making a diamond knot, as shown below. Double the diamond knot and then treble if you like.

❖ Now repeat the same knot, but this time make a big (about 500mm) loop at the other end. Check the fit of the lanyard for yourself by holding the little loop in your outstretched hand, to get the perfect length of neck loop before making the splice start. If you wish you could make an extended diamond knot by putting an extra tuck after making the crown and the wall (see page 75).

❖ By missing out the spliced start and going straight to the crown and wall round the rope, your lanyard will slide, but as I have said before, think first and watch out, it may be OK round your waist or shoulder but not round your neck.

Diamond knot/crown and wall doubled

∼ Variation: Dog lead ∼

If it is a dog lead/lanyard that you want to make, use 1.5–2m of 10mm three-strand rope and a clip. Don't forget to fit the clip before making the small loop.

FANCY *lanyard*

For something special, be it a hand-bearing compass, compact camera, bosun's call or special knife, it is good to have a lanyard that will speak silently of the skills of its maker. Long before there were certificates of competence for sailors, a man would have been judged by those little displays of skill to be seen in his knife lanyard or sea chest handles.

Today many traditional boat festivals operate a system of passes that are worn on a piece of string round the neck. I first developed this lanyard to wear my pass at the huge maritime festival held at Brest in 1992. It is not often that I have time to make something for myself, being busy making things for others; I made the 'Brest lanyard' on the ferry to France.

It has served me well ever since and has led to variations that can be used for other personal items. With a short 'tail' it suits a sports teacher's whistle or identity pass; with a longer tail it would suit a rambler's pocket compass. Make the tail longer still and your knife should not go for a swim.

MATERIALS

For a short-tailed lanyard:

* 1 x 5m of 2mm line

* 1 x 10m of 2mm line

For a long-tailed lanyard:

* 1 x 6m of 2mm line

* 12m of 2mm line

KNOTS USED

* Portuguese sennit – see page 23

* Spiral Portuguese sennit – see page 23

* Diamond knot – see pages see similar on 30-1, 72, 112

* Four-strand round sennit

* Diamond knot spliced – see page 72

* Extended diamond

METHOD

❖ Fold both pieces of line in half, seizing them together to make a pair of loops about 60mm overall and giving you four ends (two long and two short).

❖ Make a diamond knot (crown first, then wall below — see similar on pages 30-1, 72, 112) double by following round, then take hold of the seizing and work the diamond knot tight. When this has been done you will have the loops that will take the item that you don't want to lose.

❖ If you prefer only one loop at the end there are two solutions: one is that after tightening the diamond knot you could cut out the spare loop; the other, a much more seamanlike way, is to work the spare loop right down out of sight into the middle of the diamond knot.

❖ Now, with the four strands, make a length of four-strand round sennit, about 80–120mm long for a short lanyard or 350mm for a longer lanyard, as shown below. If you wish you can stop along the length of this bit of sennit and pop in another diamond knot or any other fancy four-strand knot such as a star knot or a Matthew Walker.

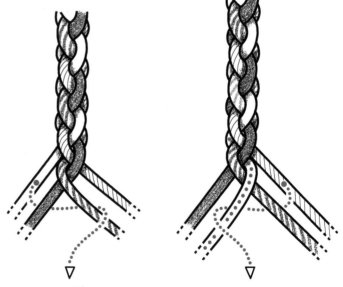

Four-strand round sennit

❖ The next part will form the neck loop. Start by making about 70–80mm of spiral Portuguese sennit, then 600mm of flat Portuguese sennit (this is the bit that actually sits round the back of your neck).

❖ Finally make another short length of spiral Portuguese sennit, this time making the twist the opposite way to the first piece of spiral sennit. You should now have four shortish tails that you can splice into the last bit of the four-strand round sennit before making a tucked diamond knot of four strands (see simple lanyard, page 70) or you can make an extended diamond knot by making one extra tuck and follow round three times.

Crown knot start
for diamond knot

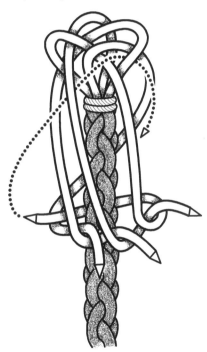

Make a wall knot below the crown, then tuck all strands as shown before doubling to make an extended diamond knot

❖ Whichever knot you choose, trim off the ends and wear your lanyard with pride.

Bosun's chair/*swing*

☞ *The old style bosun's chair with its wooden seat may in many places be replaced with the all-canvas and webbing item derived from mountaineering harnesses, but it still has a place on many traditional and commercial ships. A number of times I have been asked to make a substantial garden swing that adults can swing on with comfort and safety and have built the swing on the wooden seat of a bosun's chair.*

Whether it will be used as a bosun's chair on board ship or a garden swing, there is a proper way to reeve the suspension rope through the holes in the corners of the plank that forms the seat. The rope should cross under the plank diagonally because in the event of part of the rope wearing out, there is still some support for the seat. These diagonals also help the seat to sit level.

Chafe is the enemy of rope, and nowhere more so than in a swing, so it is a very good idea to round and fair the holes through which the rope passes before reeving the rope. All rope eyes should be protected with thimbles. People's safety is at stake, so please check for wear before using.

METHOD

❖ For both the swing and the bosun's chair, first make sure that the corners of the actual plank are well rounded to avoid damage to ship or people, and that the edges of the holes are smooth and rounded to reduce wear on the rope.

❖ I once saw an illustration of an old Dutch bosun's chair with a simple but effective carved pattern that made the seat itself less slippery and it was a joy to the eye. You may like to try something like it.

❖ For the bosun's chair, one piece of rope is reeved round in a continuous manner, with the two ends being joined under the seat with a short splice.

❖ A loop is made from the two bights of rope at the top by making a flat seizing round the four 'legs'. It is a good idea to have a thimble in this eye.

The rope should always cross under the seat.

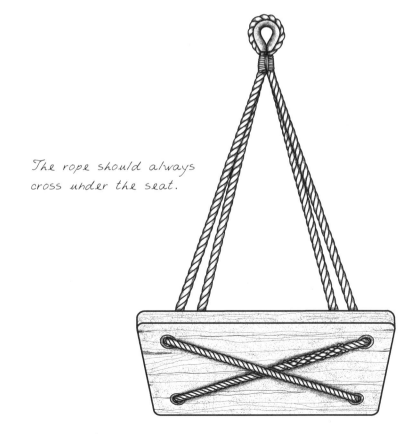

Rope HANDRAILS

☞ *In the past, manropes were ropes rigged over the side of the ship to assist people getting on board. They could be quite decorative items, one end pointed, and the other finishing in a manrope knot, sometimes known as a 'wall and crown'.*

In today's world, the manrope knot still makes the most handsome of ends to a rope handrail, whether it is in the house as a rope banister, on board ship by the companionway steps, or the rope handrails on the gangway.

The strands of the rope making the knot are first covered in canvas (although this is not essential if care is taken when tying the knot). The rope itself could also be covered with canvas and then wormed over the top and the whole thing may well have been painted in a selection of colours, to bring out the pattern of the knots. The addition of a leather star washer can also set the knot off handsomely.

Should you want an end with a tassel, make a diamond knot (a crown first, followed by a wall knot, see pages 30-1, 112) instead and tease out the yarns.

I like to make the rope handrail as tight as possible, as it will soon stretch to give a little sag. However, if you are using natural material in an area where it is likely to get wet and shrink, you must allow up to 10% for shrinkage.

Star washer

METHOD

❖ If you are going to have leather washers you must make them first. The best way of doing this is to make a cardboard template, drawing the six-pointed star with a pair of compasses. The circle that forms the outer points of the star should be about three times the diameter of the hole in the middle. Remember, rope can be a bit over its stated size. Pin this template on to the leather and use a chisel to cut out the points of the star. Finally, use a punch for the centre hole. I always do this cutting into the end grain of a block of wood.

❖ Now you can start the knots. Tape the end of the rope so it is easier to thread it through the brackets or stanchions, and fit the leather washer if you are having one. Measure the allowance for the knot and tie a constrictor knot as a temporary seizing. Unlay the strands and tape the ends.

❖ First make a wall knot, then top it with a crown knot and double the whole lot. I prefer to double below the wall and crown, rather than above.

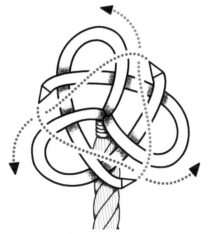

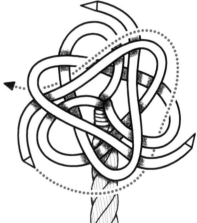

Manrope knot: first a wall knot, then a crown knot on top

Double the knot by following round with each strand as indicated

❖ Finally tuck the ends down inside the knot and trim.

❖ The result will be a handsomely finished handrail.

Cat-o'-nine-tails

⟐ *I have yet to see a true cat-o'-nine-tails from that brutal period when men could be flogged for the least infringement of discipline. There are a few descriptions, but these are hard to decipher. Most cat-o'-nine-tails in museums are someone's interpretation rather than the real thing. The truth is probably that the 'cat' was nothing very fancy, but rather just a piece of three-strand rope with a couple of knots in it to form the handle, then three strands opened out into the yarns, and these yarns laid up or plaited into lashes, the tails being knotted at the end to stop them coming undone. It was probably thrown away after use.*

The 'cat' that I describe here can easily serve as the basis of a ditty bag lanyard; just use eight tails. This cat-o'-nine-tails is more a decoration than for real use, but mounted on board it makes a fine trophy, perhaps to be awarded symbolically to the last in a race or to someone who has encouraged improvement in a team.

It starts with a Matthew Walker knot, one of my favourites. Here it is tied with nine lines, which can prove quite a handful, but it's not impossible using my method, which starts with a wall knot and grows from there. It will work for three or more strands. Try it out with three or four lines to start with and work your skill level up to the nine slowly.

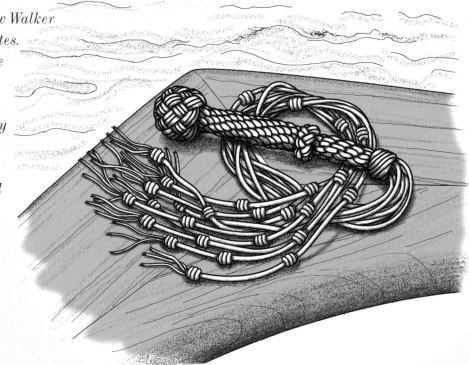

* 9 x 2.5m of 4mm line, I like to use hemp or flax

* 1 x 36mm wooden ball drilled with a hole of 4-6mm or a parrel bead

* 1 x 130mm piece of 4mm stainless steel wire rope or a nail this long with its head cut off or even a wooden dowel. This is used to stiffen the handle. It is possible to just use an extra piece of line, but it does not work so well.

KNOTS USED

* Matthew Walker knot

* Alternate crown sennit, 4+4 - see page 31

* Diamond knot/crown and wall with eight strands - see similar on pages 30-1, 72, 112

* Eight-strand crown sennit - see page 39

* Eight-strand globe knot ball covering - see page 39

METHOD

❖ Cut and measure your nine pieces of line. Make them into a bundle and put on a temporary seizing about 900mm from the end. The first 900mm will be your lashes; the rest will go to making the handle. Make a nine-strand Matthew Walker knot with the long ends. I know this will be difficult as you have to handle the long pieces of line, but when the knot is tightened it will set better for the rest of the handle.

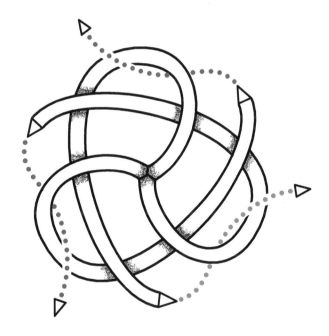

Making the Matthew Walker knot, three-strand wall knot with first series of tucks

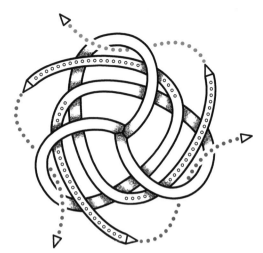

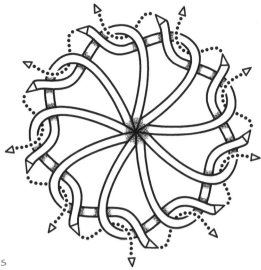

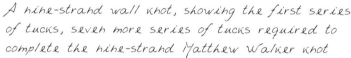

A nine-strand wall knot, showing the first series of tucks, seven more series of tucks required to complete the nine-strand Matthew Walker knot

Second series of tucks completes a full circle

❖ After the Matthew Walker has been tied, continue with the long strands, making an alternate crown sennit with four and four strands round the ninth strand which remains in the middle as a core. Make this alternate crowning for about 70mm, and then, with the same strands, make a diamond knot, still keeping the ninth strand as a core.

❖ Take whatever rod you are going to use as a stiffener and work it into the heart of the diamond knot and wrap the ninth strand round it. If the line you are using is a stranded line you can open out the lay a little so it 'grabs' the rod as it is spiralled up it.

❖ With your eight strands, cover the stiffener with an eight-strand crown sennit almost to the end, then push the wooden ball or bead over the end of your rod and use an eight-strand globe knot to cover. You will need to follow round this knot three times to cover the ball completely. Your whip handle is now complete.

❖ You can knot the ends of the lashes — some sources say there should be three knots per lash — with simple overhand knots or blood knots (overhand knots with an extra couple of tucks). This would have certainly made a brutal weapon but looks fine for decoration.

∾ VARIATION: DITTY BAG LANYARD ∾

You may prefer to make a ditty bag lanyard as it is not such a gruesome project. Make it just like the 'cat' but with eight strands, the 'tails' or strands being spliced to the eyelets at the top of the bag, and a Turk's head slide made round them to close the neck of the bag. There is no need for a stiffener in the handle. As an alternative to the globe knot, you could finish with a star knot or a second diamond knot, working a suspension loop in the manner of the finish for the binocular strap on page 86.

Tiller/boat hook COVERING

☞ *To make a good grip on a tiller, boat hook handle, mast support post, stanchion or grab handle is a simple enough job using a series of half hitches. This can be with just a single strand of line, the hitches all going in one direction, which gives a spiral effect and is known as French hitching, French whipping or grapevine service.*

If more than one strand is used there are many combinations of either direction of hitch or the number of strands used, giving many patterns. The two I show here are named Moku hitching and St Mary's hitching, and were first shown by Brion Toss in WoodenBoat *magazine about twenty years ago. They are both simple and relatively quick to do and give very distinct patterns. From these basic ideas you can experiment to create lots more patterns. Whatever style or styles of hitching you use, finish each end with a Turk's head.*

When all is done you may consider varnishing the work. This is essential if the material you have used to hitch with is natural and is likely to be exposed to the weather, as left untreated it will soon work loose. However, be careful as varnishes tend to change the colour of the line used. It is well worth experimenting, by dipping a piece of your line into the intended varnish.

Many yacht varnishes will make a flax or hemp line go very dark brown, and will turn a white line a golden colour. I have found that some of the varnishes based on either acrylic or PVA, which allow the brushes to be cleaned in water and are sometimes sold as 'low odour', only slightly darken the work.

In the past, this sort of work would have been painted, probably white, with perhaps the Turk's heads picked out in a selection of colours.

MATERIALS

* 2mm, 3mm or 4mm line: I usually use 2mm diameter line or even smaller on most handles, with perhaps 3mm or 4mm material for mast support posts. Irrespective of which method you decide to use, the amount of material required must be determined for each job by taking a metre and making a series of half hitches round the item to be covered. When the metre has all been used up, measure and see how long the piece of hitching is, divide that length into the overall length to be covered and add, say, 10% for luck. You now know how many metres you require. I usually use thicker material for the Turk's heads at each end.

* Varnish or paint if required

KNOTS USED

* Constrictor knot - see page 12
* French hitching
* Moku hitching
* St Mary's hitching
* Turk's heads of choice - see pages 44, 89-90, 100, 133

METHOD

❖ First work out the amount of material you need (see above), either as one piece for French hitching, divided into two ends for Moku hitching or divided into two-thirds and one-third for St Mary's hitching. You should then make up the line into a bundle or bundles, perhaps held with a rubber band.

French hitching: always hitch in the same direction

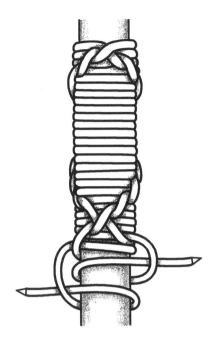

Moku hitching: hitch alternate strands in opposite directions

St Mary's hitching: always hitch the strand at the top, all hitches in the same direction

❖ Always start with a constrictor knot tied in the material, at the end for French hitching, in the middle for Moku hitching or in the middle of the longer piece and holding the short length in place for St Mary's hitching. Then you can start making your half hitches.

❖ As always, keeping an even tension is the key to good-looking work. Fine line has a tendency to cut into your hands as you tighten each hitch, so if you intend to cover a long length it would be a good idea to wear gloves or finger protection of some sort. I find a short piece of bicycle inner tube works well if the line I am using is anything but white, other people take preventative measures by wrapping some tape round the fingers that take most of the punishment.

❖ When you have finished hitching, use one of the strands to make another constrictor knot to hold the end(s) secure. Finish each end with a Turk's head covering the constrictor knot.

❖ Things can be a little more complicated if you like the idea of making a selection of hitching styles on a single piece. If in doubt, allow a little extra line to start with. Also, I find it's easier and neater to change from a method using two or three strands to one that uses fewer strands rather than adding extra strands. You may still need to cover the transition point with a Turk's head.

❖ Varnish or paint the finished job if appropriate.

BINOCULAR *strap*

Binoculars and many cameras need a strap or lanyard that has loops at both ends and will sit comfortably round the back of the neck. This strap uses the width of the Portuguese sennit to take the weight on the neck and the flexibility of four-strand round sennit for the rest of the piece. As both sides of the strap must match, it has to be worked out from the middle, giving the problem of making little loops on each end.

The principle of the solution described here was first pointed out to me by Paulo Escudeiro from Portugal, and it can easily be adapted to make loops on the ends of lanyards and other items that have four or more strands. These loops could be made directly on to the fixing rings of the binoculars, or you may wish to fit small split rings that can in turn be fitted to the fixing points.

Make the strap as long as you like, camera straps are usually longer than binocular straps, but you are the one making it so do what suits you.

MATERIALS

* ✳ 2 × 3.3m of 3mm cord

* ✳ 2 × 2m of 3mm cord

* ✳ Two split rings of about 16mm diameter are required, unless you attach directly to the camera or binoculars

KNOTS USED

* ✳ Diamond knots – see pages 72, 112

* ✳ Portuguese sennit flat – see page 23

* ✳ Spiral Portuguese sennit – see page 23

* ✳ Four-strand round sennit – see page 74

* ✳ Crown loop ends

METHOD

❖ If you start at the middle of the strap you will have to handle shorter pieces of line and so make a quicker, easier and hopefully neater job. At the middle of the two shorter pieces, temporarily tie the centre of the longer pieces, and with the long lengths of line commence flat Portuguese sennit one way.

❖ Untie your seizing and work the other way, using the other long lengths of line. You will need to make at least 150mm each way, that is, 300mm in total; you could then do a short length of twisted Portuguese sennit each end, if you wish.

❖ Do keep some symmetry to your work. At each end, make a diamond knot and double it.

❖ Now make about 250mm of four-strand round sennit each side and put on a temporary seizing to stop the sennit coming unlaid while you finish each end of the strap.

❖ First do a crown knot and then make an extra tuck to give a loop to go through the fittings on your binoculars or have a split ring put through later.

Make a loop before creating the diamond knot by making a wall knot underneath and then doubling

❖ Complete by making a diamond knot and doubling it. Then fit split rings to the ends so that your strap can be fitted to your binoculars or camera.

Covering A WHEEL

👉 *Today's stainless steel steering wheels are all very fine and strong, but they cry out for some sort of rope covering. Not just for appearance – a well-covered wheel can look very handsome indeed – but also for grip and comfort. As one of my customers said, 'When it's cold out on the North Sea that's when I feel the benefit of the rope-covered wheel. It's so much friendlier and does not freeze the hands in quite the way an uncovered wheel will.'*

To do this job properly there are a number of things to be done correctly. The first is the choice of material. Much as you may like the idea and feel of natural cordage, it is not really the right thing to use unless you then heavily varnish the wheel, which in some ways defeats the purpose. I always use a synthetic material, which will not change its tension when wet; I use nylon, polyester or a good quality multi-filament polypropylene. Do not use too thick a material; 3mm diameter is ideal.

The next decision is the actual method of covering the rim. You can use French whipping (see page 84) or Moku hitching (see page 85).

Whichever rim covering method you use, at each spoke you will get a gap. It is here that the four-lead, five-bight Turk's head made up as a three legged covering will make all the difference. This is the detail that gives a proper neat finish, covering that unsightly gap.

If when the rudder is square your centre point on the wheel is also a king spoke, make a four-lead, five-bight Turk's head out of perhaps a different colour and larger (4mm) material, so you can find it by feel, even in the darkest of nights. Alternatively you can put another Turk's head round the king spoke itself.

If the all-square point is midway between spokes you can add another style of Turk's head at this point.

One word of warning: an average wheel takes a lot of line to cover, and fine line cuts the fingers very quickly. You may find it helpful to tape up your fingers before you start to prevent blisters. Alternatively you can do the job a bit at a time when you have a few days to enjoy doing it.

MATERIALS

✳ 3mm braided nylon, polyester or a good quality multi-filament polypropylene, the quantity will need to be calculated to suit the individual wheel

✳ 2-3m of 4mm material as above to make a Turk's head at the king spoke

KNOTS USED

✳ French whipping - see page 84 or Moku hitching - see page 85

✳ Four-lead, five-bight Turk's head

METHOD

❖ Having chosen the material you wish to use, make a knot at a point 2m from the end and then make a series of half hitches round the wheel until the 2m are used up. Measure the length of the rim that has been covered and calculate from this the amount of material you will need to cover the entire rim of the wheel, adding a little bit extra to be absolutely certain of having enough.

❖ Measure off the material to be used and make it up into one bundle if you are French whipping or two equal bundles joined in the middle if you are going to use Moku hitching.

❖ Start by tying a constrictor knot round the rim at a spoke (the king spoke if you know which that is), having one half of the constrictor knot each side of the spoke. You can now carry on making your hitches with either the one or the two ends, depending on your covering method. Pull each half hitch tight.

❖ You will soon realise why I suggested that you put some tape round your fingers, or maybe you will be able to take a rest. It is best to stop at a spoke so that the tension is exactly the same for the whole section.

❖ When the complete rim has been covered, tuck the end or ends under the constrictor knot that you started with.

❖ Now neaten up each spoke junction point with a four-lead, five-bight Turk's head, probably followed round three times.

❖ Dummy up with a dozen slack turns round the rim and add a bit to get the rough amount needed for this knot. Measure the length of material used to make the first Turk's head before you start so that you can be closer in your measurement for the rest of the knots.

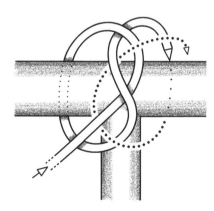

Four-lead, five-bight Turk's head start

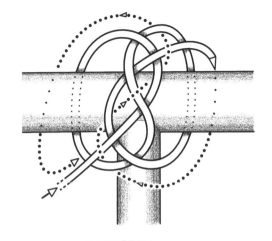

❖ Finish off with a Turk's head in 4mm line at the king spoke or centre position on the wheel. The result will be a very good-looking wheel, which is much more pleasant to hold than the cold stainless steel.

Four-lead, five-bight Turk's head ready to be doubled or trebled

~ FOUR-LEAD, THREE-BIGHT TURK'S HEAD ~

This Turk's head is based on the constrictor knot (see page 12). It is best to practise by tying it round your fingers. By splitting open the knot and making a pass round your hand and tucking under over under, you will finish up with four strands plaited together with three bights on the edge.

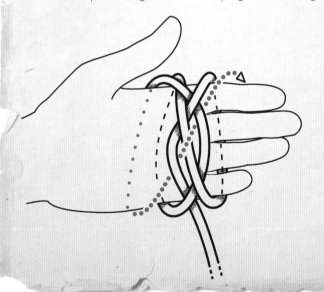

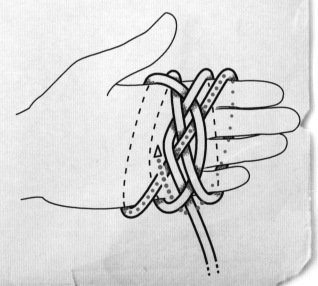

BELTS

☞ *A belt can be as simple as a piece of rope or rope yarn tied round the waist to hold up your trousers or keep your oilskin jacket closed. The late Charlie Brinkley, fisherman and ferryman from Felixstowe Ferry on the Suffolk coast, called such a belt a 'Board of Trade belt', a reflection on the probable source of the material.*

A casual arrangement like this can be improved by making up a piece of sennit. I have a dressing gown belt, made during the Second World War, that is cotton string made up as eight-strand square sennit (see page 38), with the ends finished as tassels and dyed, perhaps, in permanent blue ink.

A far more advanced belt can be made using Portuguese sennit, or square knotting, one of the main ingredients for all macramé. Belts like this were a favourite item for sailors to make; fine fancy ones in colour for a girl at home, white ones to be traded with an officer for a favour, or just for their own use.

I will give you the essentials of a plain and simple belt, how to start and finish, with plain square knotting in between. For further decoration use colour, or variations of knots that can be found in The Ashley Book of Knots *or macramé books.*

MATERIALS

* A belt buckle of your choice

* Some fine line, preferably quite hard-laid, 1-2mm diameter. It is difficult to specify how many lengths of material will be needed as this will depend on the width of the buckle and how many square knots can be tied side by side to make that width. This must be worked out by making up a small sample piece.

* The length of the individual pieces of line will depend on the length of the belt. When square knotting you need the lengths to be four to five times the finished length. As we start at the point of the belt with the line doubled back, the actual pieces of line will be about nine times the finished belt length. To make a belt approximately 1.2m long, you will need to cut your line in ten- to twelve-metre lengths.

KNOTS USED

* Portuguese sennit/square knotting - see page 23

METHOD

❖ I always start at the shaped end of the belt and finish at the buckle, as it is so much easier to hide the ends behind the buckle and the pointed end is the part that is handled the most, so needs to be strong and neat. For the start it helps to have some pins and a piece of soft board, such as insulating board, a thick cork tile, a piece of soft foam covered with cloth or even a cushion or pillow, but it is possible to work it in your hands.

❖ Start by middling two pieces of line, folding them back on themselves. Make the first piece of Portuguese sennit or square knotting by tying the outer two strands round the middle two strands. Then place two more middled pieces of line either side of your first square knot and with two of the ends from the first knot and two new ends make another square knot, first one side of the initial knot and repeat the other, thus making new square knots either side of the first, as shown below.

The shaped end start, shown open for clarity, but all knots should be pulled up snug

❖ Carry on linking the square knots and adding in extra pairs of line until the required width is reached. You can now keep up the square knotting for the entire length of the belt. Make sure that each row is the same, and that you make every square knot the same way.

❖ When you reach the buckle, bring the ends round the bar of the buckle and tie them off with a square knot round themselves, with the ends at the back of the belt buckle, tucked back, parallel with the core strands of the last couple of pieces of the Portuguese sennit, as shown below. For some materials you may feel that a little touch of glue will help to hold any loose ends in place.

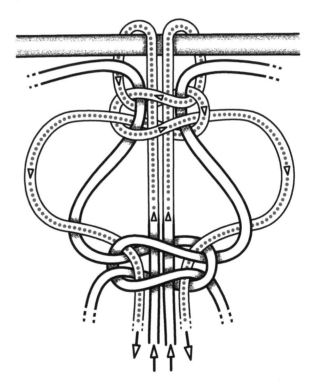

The finish at the buckle from the back, shown open for clarity, but all knots should be pulled up snug

GROMMETS *for quoits, blocks and sea chest beckets*

☞ An endless circle of rope called a grommet can be made from a single strand of three-strand rope just over three times the length of the finished ring. This ring or grommet is the essential ingredient for a game of deck quoits or a strop for a wooden block. A pair will make simple sea chest handles or beckets, which when decorated with worming, leather and Turk's heads add a great deal of style, telling the world that this chest belongs to a real 'marlinespike sailor'.

However they are used, the skill is to get the size correct and then to make the join in such a way as barely to increase the diameter of the rope. This join is the same as that used in a long splice. There are many variations of making it, with each one having its proponents, advantages and disadvantages, each in their way correct; hence the saying 'different ships, different long splices'.

Whatever the variation of join used, it helps a great deal if the rope used keeps its form when unlaid. Most natural fibres are fine, but cotton can be a little tricky, while among the synthetics nylon can give problems. All can be used, but the difficult ones need special care.

As one piece of three-strand rope will provide enough strands to make three grommets, deck quoits are usually made up as sets of three. If you have single and double blocks to strop, always cut the rope long enough to make the biggest strop. When making a pair of beckets, make three and use the best pair.

MATERIALS

For a set of three quoits:

* 3m of 18mm or 24mm diameter three-strand rope, natural if possible

For a pair of chest beckets:

* 3m of 14mm or 16mm diameter three-strand hemp or manila, if possible

* 8m fine tarred marline to worm the rope

* The same or larger to make the Turk's heads

* Two pieces of leather, approximately 75mm x 150mm

For block strops:

* One piece of three-strand rope three times the circumference of the strop, plus about 300mm

KNOTS USED

For all:

* Grommet

* Long splice join

For chest beckets:

* Worming

* Turk's heads of choice - see pages 44, 89-90, 100, 133

METHOD

❖ Having worked out how much rope is required, form a circle in the middle of the rope with the ends overlapping. Mark both parts of the rope at this cross over point.

❖ Now gently unlay one strand from the rope, taking great care to keep as much of the twist, kink and lay in the strand as possible. It helps to hold the rope up and let the strand that is being unlaid hang down. When you have the strand free, form a circle with the marks of the cross over side by side.

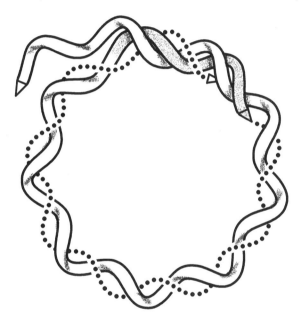

Forming a grommet

❖ Gently lay one end of the strand round itself, starting to reform the structure of the original rope. As the strand is laid into the kink of the lay, it may help to give a slight twist to the strand to put back any lost lay. When most of one end of the strand has been used up, use the other end of the strand to complete the three-strand structure, again gently adding a bit of a twist and perhaps a bit of a push to get the strand to sit neatly.

❖ When a complete circle of rope has been made, the two ends will overlap. These ends are now joined to give the least increase in diameter possible. Tuck the end as shown, taking a bit of the twist out of the strand as you do. If you tuck correctly the strands should bed down neatly; if you have tucked the wrong way it will stand proud no matter how hard you pull and push.

❖ Now tuck each end under one against the lay, leave out half of the strand end and repeat. When all ends are neatly tucked the grommet can be stretched round a large fid (if you have got one big enough) or just stretched into a good shape, before trimming the ends.

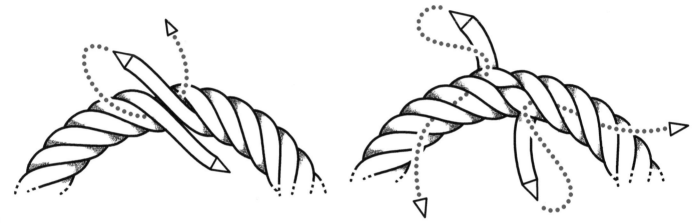

The long splice finish

❖ Do not trim too tight because any strain could cause the ends to pop untucked. A more sophisticated join starts with halving each strand end before making the initial tuck. Make the second and third grommet using the other two strands.

❖ Another way to get similar sized grommets that works very well for quoits uses circles of garden wire or similar material measured to a standard length, marked and twisted to join at the mark. Use these rings of wire as a base round which to twist and lay up your rope strand in a manner similar to the above. The wire can be left in the grommets to give a degree of stiffness to the quoits.

❖ Two grommets can be used as they are for the most basic of sea chest handles or beckets, or they can be easily decorated by taking a single piece of marline and laying it into the groove of the rope; this is called 'worming' the rope. The marline goes round and round, finally meeting the other end, where it can be knotted and the ends tucked out of sight.

❖ A piece of leather can be added where the grommet passes under the cleat of the chest. Turk's heads can be added for still more decoration.

Pair of FANCY SPLICED CHEST BECKETS

The simplest of rope handles for a chest can be made from a piece of rope short-spliced together to form a circle. The short splice gives a greater diameter to the rope and is therefore more comfortable to the hands when lifting a heavy chest. Add a little decoration to this style of handle by making the splice with extra long ends. Rather than trimming them at each end of the splice, these ends are used to make diamond knots round the body of the rope. Chest beckets made like this are quick to do but still have a bit of style. You can, of course, go on and add Turk's heads etc. to your heart's content.

MATERIALS

* ✹ 2 × 1.7m of 10mm or 12mm three-strand rope

KNOTS USED

* ✱ Short splice

* ✱ Diamond knot - see page 112

METHOD

❖ Decide how large a circle of rope you wish to finish up with, which will probably be something like 600mm in circumference.

❖ Before commencing the splice, things can be made easier for tucking by taping or whipping the ends of each individual strand. Unlay both ends of the rope equally and marry these ends by butting the strands together to form a circle of the size you want.

❖ Make one tuck with each strand against the lay of the rope in the normal manner. Repeat for the other handle, checking that they are of the same circumference. Tuck each side of the splice two or three more times. Check that both sets of beckets are the same.

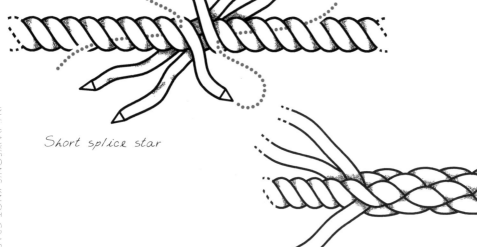

Short splice star

Short splice with ends ready to make diamond knots

❖ With the long tails left, make first a crown knot round the body of the rope and then a wall knot beneath it, double the crown and then the wall, tucking the ends up through the middle of the diamond knot.

❖ Work each of the strands tight and trim.

Turk's heads *for decoration or napkin rings*

Turk's heads are found all over the world in many cultures and are often vested with mystical significance. They come in all sorts of sizes and complexity. They are beautiful knots that provide decoration and a practical purpose when used as grips, splash barriers and protection against chafe and knocks, or as a purely decorative binding. I find that there are a few that will be useful time and again to cover joins and ends when covering handles with hitching. The odd Turk's head on the handle of a tool gives a sign of ownership, in just the same way that Herman Melville had his pipe made taboo on a Pacific island in the 1840s.

The best way of describing Turk's heads is that they are a continuous plaited ring made with a single strand of line. This single strand version may be followed round as many times as you wish, usually two, three or four times. They should not be confused with the manrope knot or diamond knot, both of which are made with the strands of a rope, nor with the monkey's fist, which is tripled, quadrupled etc. as it is made.

To help differentiate between the various Turk's heads we call the number of loops on its edge 'bights' and the number of strands that make up the plait 'leads'. There are many variations of 'bights' and 'leads', but early in the twentieth century it was independently discovered by CW Ashley, GH Taber and LG Miller that a true Turk's head cannot be made where the leads and the bights have a common divisor; you can make a three-lead, four-bight and a three-lead, five-bight but not a three-lead, six-bight Turk's head. JC Turner and AG Schaake have recently proven the reason for this mathematically in New Zealand.

Whole books have been written about Turk's heads and some people get totally hooked on tying ever more complex variations. There are lots of different ways of setting about tying them. They can be tied round the fingers and slipped over the item to be covered and they can be tied in much the same way directly round the object.

❖ To make your Turk's heads into napkin rings, tie them in 3mm hard cord round empty 35mm film cases. To stiffen them, give them a coating of PVA glue mixed with water 50:50, let them dry, slide off the case, trim the ends inside and paint inside with more of the PVA glue and water mix.

❖ Here is another Turk's head that you may find useful. The five-lead, four-bight can be tied round your fingers. Follow the diagrams, using your thumb to hold the various passes in place. The earlier passes will lay out a pattern that can be locked into a full over-under design by the last full pass round the fingers.

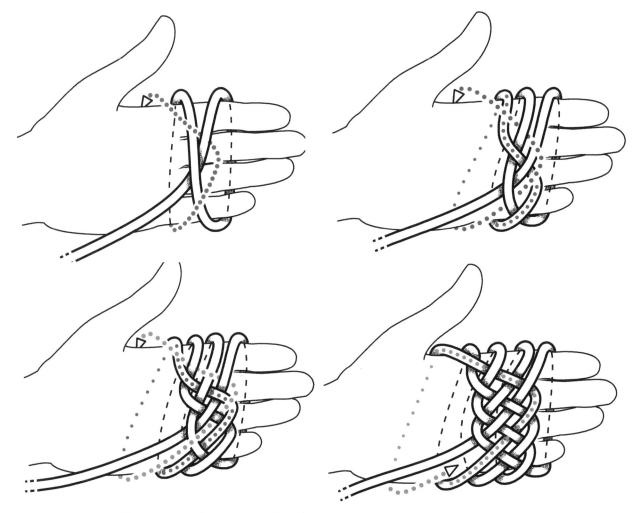

Five-lead, four-bight Turk's head: step by step

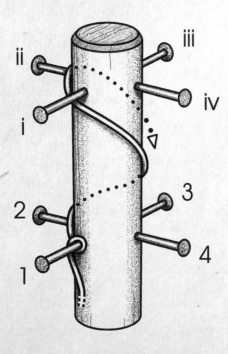

Turk's head gadget

❖ More complex Turk's heads require different approaches. One is to put pins in a rod as shown, and wrap a fine line round and round from one end to the other, making a dummy pattern and not worrying about the overs and unders. With this basic network complete, use it as a guide to follow and create the overs and unders as required.

❖ It is possible to tie directly round the gadget by following formulae. These can get very complicated, but here are some simple ones that I first saw in Quinton Winch's book *Nets and Knots*.

❖ Make up a rod with two sets of four pins or pegs in it, as shown in the illustration, one set of pegs to be numbered 1–4, the other to be numbered I, II, III, IV.

❖ Starting at peg 1, take your line right round the rod to peg II, round and back to the left-hand side peg 2, going over and over each time the line crosses the line already in position. Go round back again to the right-hand side, going over and over to peg number III. Go from peg III round to peg 3, going under, over, under, over. From peg 3 go round to peg IV, going under, over, under, over. From IV go to 4 going over, under, over, over, under. From 4 round to I, going over, under, o, o, u, o, and finally complete the full circuit by returning to 1 by going u, o, u, o, u, o, u, o. Having completed the Turk's head, take out the pins before doubling or trebling. This is all shown in the diagrams below.

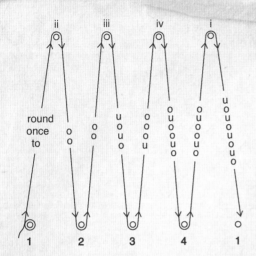

Formula for nine-lead, four-bight Turk's head

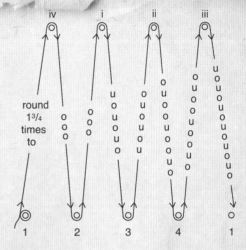

Formula for thirteen-lead, four-bight Turk's head

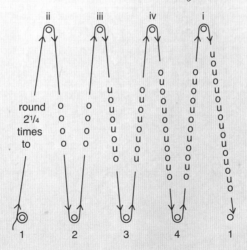

Formula for seventeen-lead, four-bight Turk's head

❖ These long complex Turk's heads make an ideal covering for a knife handle. In fact, there are many things you can put a Turk's head on. Perhaps you will catch the Turk's head fever just as they did on the Brendan Voyage in the Seventies, where 'every item that could possibly be embellished with a Turk's head was duly decorated' (see Tim Severin, *The Brendan Voyage*).

KNOT *boards*

It is difficult to trace the actual origin of knot boards, but I think that they were made either as a training aid on board ship or in a naval training establishment, or as a demonstration of the tyer's skill, to be either displayed in a rigging loft or chandler's or perhaps given away as a gift. Some were made up to be the basis of the illustrations of knot books. Today they are to be found everywhere, many being mass-produced almost on a production line. I have never wanted to mass produce knot boards, preferring to aim at the special 'work of art'.

There is a certain satisfaction on completing a well balanced layout with examples of one's skills and knowledge, perhaps with a theme or some special appropriate knots for the person you are making it for. Making your own gives you the opportunity to demonstrate your skills and make something individual – a work of art. You can take that extra hour to make a very intricate hitched bottle to act as a centre piece. You can make your board have a special theme, knots for climbers, fishermen, true lovers or maybe just loop knots. I have seen fine boards that show the rigging of tackles, others with a selection of lashings, yet others showing each stage of making a selection of knots and splices.

METHOD

❖ The first thing to decide is how big you want your board to be, and then what frame to use and whether to glaze. Get your frame first, or else you may find that there is nothing deep enough to take that extra special thing you want to put in.

❖ Frames are always difficult and expensive to buy, I have big ones (600mm x 900mm) specially made by a joiner, with a deep moulding and fillet strip. I stain and polish them myself. They are a major expense. Small frames can be made up by a picture framer; perhaps you will be lucky to find a sympathetic one who can supply a good deep moulding. The drawings give some ideas as to the variations possible.

❖ The fillet strip holds the glass in place, and means that it is possible for the board to be shipped and have the glass fitted later. It also means that in the event of an accident the broken glass can be replaced.

❖ For a backing board I usually use 9mm plywood covered with felt. I fix the knots with brass pins bought from the model shop. Pins through felt enable you to move and reposition, without a hole showing. I hold the pins with a pair of needle-nosed pliers, and hammer them in with a pin hammer.

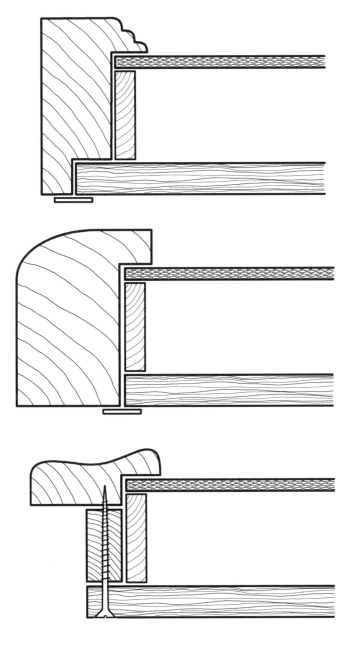

❖ I always feel that it is the layout that matters. It helps if there is one special piece of work that acts as a focus. I like to show the knots at work where possible, that is, bends joining together, hitches to a rod. I only use 'bits of brass' etc. to show the working of a knot, for example a block on a thump mat or a miniature bosun's call on a miniature lanyard.

❖ For the knots you can use any material you like. I prefer to use either flax or cotton, varying the size for different knots, usually using 3mm for the main knots and the same or possibly smaller for the mats, the finest line I can get to hitch a miniature bottle, about 1.5mm if I do some decorative hitching round a rod. The Turk's heads round that rod can be in 2mm or 2.5mm.

❖ Splices need to be made in larger material to be seen, so use 6mm or 8mm rope. It looks best if all the ends are whipped. I use the finest waxed whipping twine, occasionally using coloured twine, perhaps to match the felt background.

❖ Naming the knots is another problem to be solved, individual brass tags are expensive and it can be cheaper to buy in bulk, but you are then restricted to the same knots. You could use a computer to generate your labels or handwrite them. I stick these labels in place with polystyrene cement. Test your glue on a scrap piece of felt and paper first.

❖ Don't forget to sign and date your finished knot board. One day it will be a piece of history.

Constructing a knot board

Monkey's fist LIGHT PULL

Among sailors the monkey's fist is known the world over. It is the knot found on the end of a heaving line. The weight of this handsome knot helps the heaving line to travel further and more accurately. The monkey's fist has a special significance to the sailor as his first connection with the land and his helping friend when needing assistance.

It is often confused with the Turk's head but, unlike the Turk's head, it is always spherical in shape and its method of construction is totally different; the full number of passes being defined as it is made. It cannot be enlarged after it has been tied.

It helps to have something round in the centre to give it shape. This can be a wooden ball or a knot tied in the end of the line and built up with a little yarn to make a ball. In the past it was often a pebble or a bolt or lump of lead, although a dock worker taking a heaving line with what he considered to be a dangerously heavy monkey's fist would cut it off. Today putting a weight in a heaving line i s considered to contravene all the safety at work rules.

A good use of the monkey's fist in the home is to make a light pull or blind pull.

METHOD

❖ If you are using the 4mm line as a suspension line, add the length of drop you want to the above measurements and start making the monkey's fist round the ball.

❖ You will need to make seven passes or circles on each face of the knot. Use your fingers to make and keep the series of wrappings in some sort of order. Insert the ball after making only two of the final series of passes, then carry on to complete the seven passes with the ball inside.

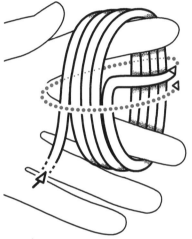

Use your fingers to keep the series of wrappings in order

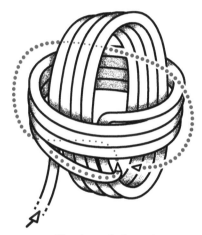

Route of final passes

Put centre 'ball' in before completing final passes

❖ When the knot has been tied loosely, work all your slack to the longest end, which will be your suspension line. Trim the short end to about 10mm and tuck it into the body.

❖ If you feel that 4mm line is too heavy as a suspension line, it is possible to drill a 3mm hole through a wooden ball with a countersunk hole of about 5mm one end, thread a thin line of perhaps 2mm through it and knot the end so that it does not pull out but is buried in the countersunk hole. Then cover the ball with a monkey's fist, trimming the ends short and burying them inside.

Monkey's fist DOOR STOP

☞ *Tying the monkey's fist in the normal way leaves two ends. If a loop is required on the monkey's fist, one end can be formed into an eye and spliced or knotted into a loop, or the ends could be spliced together. To my mind, neither of these options is very neat, especially if you wish to make a small monkey's fist key ring.*

I first worked out a neat and secure method of making a monkey's fist with a loop when commissioned to make floating monkey's fist key rings, using a table tennis ball as a core. The previous maker had just tucked one end inside, held in place by a dab of glue. It looked neat, but, of course, it soon pulled out. To resolve this problem, I introduced a loop by a slight deviation from the usual pattern of turns.

After making hundreds, if not thousands, of these I wanted to make something much bigger that would show off the sculptural form of this special knot. Using 18mm manila, I made the monkey's fist in the same special way, but with a core made up from scrap lead, folded and beaten into shape and then covered with a little spun yarn to prevent the rope becoming soiled as the knot was worked tight.

These door stops have proved very popular, and are sculptures in their own right. This exact design can be made into a fender by substituting the ball of lead and spun yarn for a ball of old corks and spun yarn. Whatever the scale of your monkey's fist, be it for earrings, key rings, light pulls, Christmas tree decorations, fenders or doorstops, you can be certain that if you use this monkey's fist deviation the loop will never pull out.

MATERIALS

For a door stop:

* Scrap lead made up into a ball about 65-70mm in diameter, then covered with scrap yarn to bring it up to 100-115mm in diameter

* 8m of 18mm rope will cover with four passes. I like the look of three-strand rope for this sculptural project.

For the floating key ring:

* One table tennis ball

* 4m of 6mm rope will cover with five passes. I prefer to use polypropylene, either as a hemp lookalike or in the coloured multi-filament form, as polypropylene is one of the few ropes that floats

KNOTS USED

* Monkey's fist with a deviation

METHOD

❖ It is probably a good idea to start with a key ring version first. This gives you the chance to understand how this monkey's fist deviates from the standard one without having to struggle with the problem of working with heavy 18mm rope as well.

❖ The start is as for the standard monkey's fist: first five passes round your fingers, then five more passes at right angles round the first set, then tuck the working end diagonally through the centre, out the other side, form a loop and tuck the final series of passes from the other side.

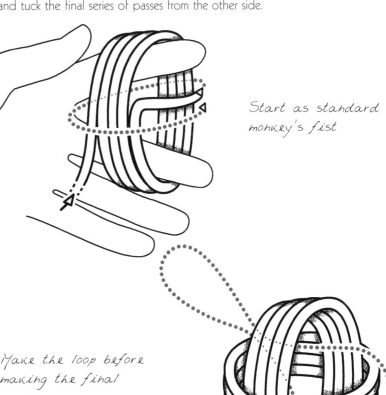

Start as standard monkey's fist

Make the loop before making the final passes

❖ Put the ball in the middle after just two of these last passes, then complete as shown below, trapping the ball inside. The whole knot can be worked tight in the usual manner. It is a little tricky following the hidden diagonal pass out to the loop and back again, but with care it can be done.

Put centre 'ball' in before completing final passes

❖ When you are happy with your knot, cut the ends off, leaving about 15mm and tuck them into the knot. When you have mastered this, you can tackle 18mm rope to make a doorstop.

❖ Heavy rope needs a slightly different approach. You will need to build it up loosely in your hand, using the stiffness of the rope to give some shape to the passes. Put your yarn-covered weight in the middle and complete the final set of passes.

❖ I have allowed plenty of material but, even so, you may be slightly short on the first loose tying of the knot. You should gently tighten the knot from the beginning, bringing the slack right through the knot to give you enough rope to complete all four of your last passes.

❖ Adjust the knot so that all is neat, although a little loose. Now work it properly tight. For this I use a big Swedish fid to lever out a loop which I take in one hand and with a hammer in the other hand, give a few glancing blows to force through the last of any slack. Working the monkey's fist tight in this way should give you a tight hard knot.

❖ When you are satisfied that you have the knot as tight and even as you wish, the two tails can be heaved even tighter using a heaving mallet or heaver (see page 8) before trimming off flush. When all this has been done I hammer the knot into shape, making it slightly flat at the bottom. You now have a handsome piece of sculpture that will act as a fine door stop.

Sailor's WHISK

 *Sailors would swab the decks daily using giant swabs made from old rope (see page 113). They would wash the dishes with a miniature version of the deck swab. The table in the fo'c'sle would be kept clean with a whisk made from an odd end of rope. There are a number of ideas as to how these would look in* The Ashley Book of Knots.

This design is based on a whisk brought to me from Nova Scotia. The actual whisk is quickly tied, but it takes a while to unlay and comb out the yarns. It should be made from a hard fibre rope such as manila or sisal. I usually use 18mm manila; anything smaller is a bit on the mean side.

I have made them with 24mm rope, but the combing time is much longer. Once I made a giant whisk in 48mm sisal; it took ages to comb out but looked very handsome.

METHOD

❖ Fold the rope in half, making a loop about 100mm long by putting on a constrictor knot as a temporary seizing. This will be the handle.

❖ Unlay the strands of the rope and, with two strands from each side, make a four-strand crown knot with the two remaining strands in the middle. Follow with a wall knot under the crown and tuck the ends up through the middle, so making a diamond knot. Tighten the diamond knot, taking care not to pull the two lazy strands in the middle, as that tends to distort the lay of the rope in the handle loop.

Tying a wall knot and crown knot to make a diamond knot

❖ Untie your temporary seizing. Unlay all six strands to the yarns and then unlay all the yarns down to the fibres. This takes time and can make quite a mess, so best not do it over a clean carpet.

❖ Use a marlinespike to comb out any difficult yarns. Now wet the teased-out fibres and comb them as straight as possible. As I make a lot of these whisks, I have made up a kind of coarse comb with some nails in a piece of wood.

❖ Start by combing out the ends and working back towards the knot to comb out all the fibres. The wet yarns are much easier to comb than if they had been left dry. When you are satisfied with the combing out, tie a constrictor knot round the fibres about 130mm from the diamond knot and cut off the ends of the fibres.

❖ Slide the constrictor knot off the end and hang the whisk up to dry. Finally shake the ends to loosen any odd stray fibres and you have got a fine little whisk.

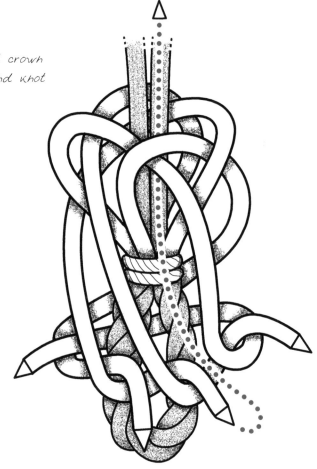

Swabs

👉 *Swabbing the deck down each morning keeps everything clean and shipshape. More importantly, if the deck is swabbed down with sea water, not only will a wooden deck be kept from shrinking in the heat of the day, but the salt in the sea water will help to pickle the timber. The benefits of salt water are well worth remembering when being tempted by a handy quayside hose, providing fresh water, which will not have the pickling effect, but if anything the exact opposite.*

Swabs are easy to make. Either a bundle of long rope yarns folded over, with a seizing round the fold to form an eye, through which would be spliced a lanyard to allow it to be dunked over the side, or a somewhat similar kind of arrangement with the yarns fixed to a wooden handle. A scaled-down swab, made the same way as a wooden-handled deck swab, will make a fine swab for washing the dishes.

MATERIALS

For a wooden-handled deck swab:

* A piece of heavy wooden broom stick 800-1000mm long

* Hemp is ideal for the deck swab, but you can use either manila or sisal

* Plenty of yarns from 18-24mm three-strand hemp, manila or sisal rope - be generous with your material

* Fine line for the seizings and whippings

For a dish swab:

* A piece of wooden dowel, 15-22mm diameter and about 350mm long

* Cotton rope gives the best results for the dish swab. I do not think synthetic cordage is good for this job

* Yarns from 8-12mm three-strand cotton rope

* Fine line for the seizings and whippings

KNOTS USED

* Constrictor knot - see page 12

* Snaked whipping

METHOD

❖ When making your swab on a wooden handle, make a couple of grooves round the end of the handle and lay the yarns lengthways around the two grooves. Tie a constrictor knot round the yarns, pulling the constrictor knot tight so as to pull the yarns into the upper groove in the handle; perhaps add a few more turns with your binding and finish off with a couple of half hitches right round the bundle.

❖ Fold down the upper yarns over your initial seizing and wrap tightly round with fine line to make a whipping, pulling the whole bundle of yarns into the lower groove. The whipping looks good if you snake it for decoration.

Snaked whipping

❖ The snaked whipping is just like a plain or simple whipping, but is finished off with a series of hitches catching one or two of the strands round the outer edge; this gives a little more protection to the whipping and adds a fine decorative touch. You will need to use a needle or Swedish fid to make the hitches; finish off by using the needle or a loop tool to bury the end deeply inside the main part of the whipping.

❖ When all is done, trim the ends of the yarns to give a neat end to the swab.

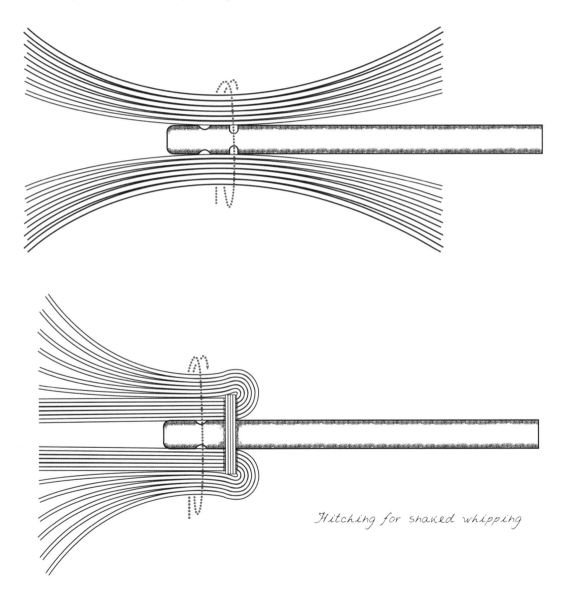

Hitching for snaked whipping

Baggywrinkle

☞ *Baggywrinkle – now there is a word to ponder. Just what is the origin of this term that describes the shaggy collection of rope yarns applied to parts of the standing rigging in order to stop chafe (the enemy of sails and running rigging)? I cannot find any reference to the use of this word, or any of its variations (bag-a-wrinkle, boogy winkles, baggy winkles, bagy wrinkles), until the twentieth century; yet chaffing gear of various sorts has been around for a very long time. Perhaps it came into being with the advent of wire standing rigging as it is possible that earlier chaffing gear was fixed to masts and spars, rather than hemp standing rigging which would tend to rot under a moisture retaining collection of rope yarns. Whatever its origins, it does the job.*

Because of how it is made, baggywrinkle is sometimes called 'railroad sennit'. Indeed it could be said that baggywrinkle is made from this material.

Making it in useful quantities is quite time-consuming. Why not call a party and get your friends to race one another to obtain a decent quantity of the stuff?

The late Tom Berry, a mat maker from Appledore in North Devon, used baggywrinkle stitched round the outside of a rope mat to give an interesting border, and there is no reason why you should not do the same.

It will also make a fine mane on a dummy horse for the 'poor old horse' ceremony, held by sailors when they have worked their pay advance and have progressed to earning actual wages.

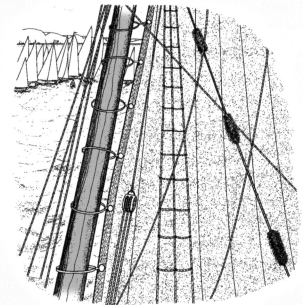

* Plenty of tarred marline 2-3mm in diameter or synthetic line of a similar size. You do not want this to rot

* Offcuts of three- or four-strand rope, cut to lengths of 150-300mm, depending on how bushy you want your baggywrinkle

* Historically it would have been made of a natural fibre; hemp is fairly soft and manila and sisal are a little stiffer. However, there is no reason why you should not use a synthetic. Your choice of fibre may depend on what old stuff you can lay your hands on. It is, of course, fine to use new rope, but it seems a bit of a waste unless the end user demands new rope.

KNOTS USED

* Overhand or thumb knot

* Tucked thrum, based on the form of the cow hitch

METHOD

❖ To make your short pieces of line or 'thrums', unlay the rope into its strands and then, if you want, unlay again down to the yarns.

❖ Take two lengths of, say, 4–6m of the marline, put them side by side and tie them together, perhaps 300m from the end. This will be the tail to attach your baggywrinkle to the shroud.

❖ Stretch this fairly tight between two fixed points, such as stanchions, posts or hooks. The points can be less than 4m apart if one end has the extra yarn wrapped round it. Put a piece of wood with a notch at both ends between this pair of lines to keep them apart, and aid with the tucking of the thrums.

❖ Lay the thrum underneath the pair of lines, pull the ends up to get the middle, then tuck them both down between the pair of lines.

Tuck rope yarns down the middle

❖ Push up tight to the knot and repeat, and repeat and repeat, to make your railroad sennit. Keep on until you have enough (you will need plenty), then release the finished piece and tie off tightly. You can now wrap the furry strip round and round your shroud, making a fine bushy set of baggywrinkles to save your sail from damage or stitch it round the outside of a mat to give that extra something.

Wrap the baggywrinkle tightly round the rigging

Bowsprit NET

A bowsprit net gives any vessel an air of importance. It serves two very useful purposes: it provides a safe platform for anyone working out on the bowsprit and it helps to stop foresails/headsails, especially the larger ones, from getting dragged in the water when being dropped and doused.

As is always the case in these matters, there are a number of ways to make the item. While some favour the usual diamond mesh approach that uses the sheet bend, just like a piece of fishing net, this can be difficult with larger sizes of rope and is not so easy to shape.

The other approach, which I prefer, is to make the net with a square mesh. Using this construction, the crossing ropes are tucked and knotted, and the whole net has a heavier 'boltrope', with meshes being formed from separate lengths of slightly smaller rope. These smaller ropes join the outer 'boltrope' with a neat right-angle splice.

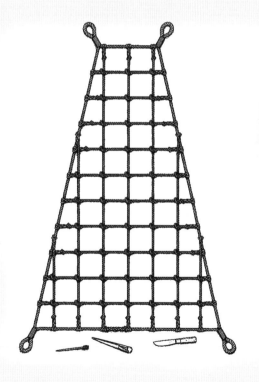

On certain vessels the net can be made directly on to the bowsprit shrouds, the ends of the meshes finishing with eye splices that are then seized to the shrouds. The whole net can be quite a complex piece, so it is well worth drawing out to scale what is intended before starting on the job.

MATERIALS

* ✱ *The amount of material depends very much on the size of the net, the size of the mesh and the thickness of the rope used. It is best to draw out the net on paper and calculate the rope required, allowing plenty for the knots and splices (it is always more than you would expect). The rope needs to be three-strand rope. As a guide for a net of, say, 4-5m long, I would suggest 8mm or 10mm for the mesh ropes and 12-14mm for the boltrope.*

KNOTS USED

* ✱ *Right-angle splice*
* ✱ *Possibly a short splice to join the boltrope - see page 98*
* ✱ *Flat seizings to make eyes at the corners on the boltrope - see page 43 - or perhaps an eye splice - see page 71*
* ✱ *Start of an eye splice as a side splice - see page 71*
* ✱ *Tuck and knot net knot*

METHOD

❖ Take some measurements from the vessel to decide what size and shape you need. You will need to make the net slightly undersized to allow for both the stretch of the rope and the tightening of the knots, because however tight you pull the knots there will still be some gain when they are put under strain.

❖ After drawing out the net on paper the net needs to be laid out full size, either on the lawn where I use six-inch nails to peg out the boltrope, or on a wooden floor using awls to hold the boltrope in place. Make any corner eyes, by either seizing or splicing, if they are wanted.

❖ With the boltrope in place, splice the long lengths to the narrow end of the boltrope using the right-angle splice, pin them in position and stretch them out. Add other long lines to the side boltrope using the start of an eye splice.

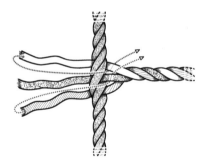

Start by first tucking the strands into the side rope in this sequence: under 2, under 1, under 2

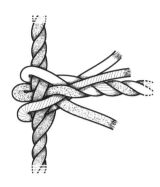

Then tuck all back. The third strand is tucked behind so that each strand is tucked over two strands of the 'boltrope'

Complete by splicing back

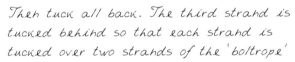

❖ It is important to space the lines out evenly. I often make up a hardboard template to act as a measure, or sometimes make the mesh the size of the Swedish fid that I am using.

❖ Next, splice one end of one of the shorter lengths to one side, pin in position and make the knots across the body of the net, as shown below. When you reach the other side of the net, right-angle splice into the boltrope. Keep on in this manner splicing side ropes in and making the meshes, keeping an eye on the shape.

knot net knot

❖ It helps to peg out as much as possible so that the net does not distort. When all the side lengths have been spliced and knotted, make a short splice in the fourth side of the boltrope and right-angle splice in the long lengths. Your net is now ready for action.

❖ Your bowsprit net also can be a very special place to relax in when the boat is behaving well on a beautiful warm sunny day.

Dog *leads*

Any nautical dog should have an appropriately stylish lead (or should that be a lanyard or tow rope?). As a member of the crew, they should reflect well on the ship and wear a good seamanlike lead.

There are a number of solutions, the simplest being a length of rope with a loop spliced one end and the other spliced to the snap shackle, clip or ring. Even this simplest of solutions can be easily lifted if, instead of a plain eye-spliced hand loop, the eye is spliced with the 'splice and diamond knot eye' (see page 72). This decorative knot feels really good in the hand.

The snap shackle can be attached with an eye splice – nicely tapered, of course – but a neater job is based on the back splice, with the eye of the shackle being held in place with the crown knot that starts the back splice. This use of the back splice is a neat way to fit snap shackles on the boat as well. A plain rope lead can be further decorated with a couple of Turk's heads tied round the main part of the rope.

However, should you wish your sea dog to have something more tiddly (fancy), then why not make the lead from four-strand round sennit interspersed with as many Matthew Walker, diamond knots and extended diamond knots as you fancy, maybe followed by a bit of crown sennit and finished off with a hand loop from flat Portuguese sennit.

MATERIALS

* Sea and land dogs of course come in various sizes, so you must judge the scale of material suitable for the dog in question as well as how long you like your lead to be. The amounts quoted here are for 1-1.2m long, so allow more if you want a longer lead

* For the plain dog lead, 2-2.5m of three-strand rope, between 8mm and 12mm, would suit most animals and their owners

* For the decorative dog lead, 1 x 6m and 1 x 9m of 4mm rope for a medium to large dog or of 3mm for a very small dog should be plenty

* A clip or snap shackle - be sure to check that it will work on your dog's collar

KNOTS USED

For the plain lead:

* Back splice starting with a crown knot

* Splice and diamond knot eye, crown and wall - see page 72

For the fancy lead:

* Diamond knot - see pages 72, 112

* Constrictor knot - see page 12

* Four-strand round sennit - see page 68

Optional:

* Matthew Walker - see page 81

* Portuguese flat sennit - see page 23

* Extended diamond - see page 75

METHOD

❖ Always start at the clip end so that you can check the length that suits you and your dog before making the loop that forms the handle.

❖ The simple lead is straightforward: make the crown knot so that it captures the clip and then make a couple of complete tucks before tapering the splice by dropping yarns out of each strand as you tuck.

❖ The handle end can be a plain eye splice, or start as an eye splice then make a crown and wall and double them.

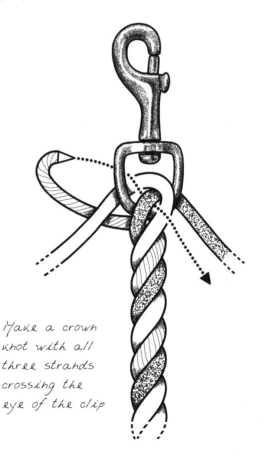

Make a crown knot with all three strands crossing the eye of the clip

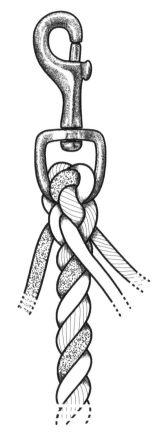

Complete by splicing back

∾ VARIATION: FANCY DOG LEAD ∾

❖ The fancy lead is again started at the clip. Put the clip in the middle of the two lengths of line, temporarily seized in place, to give you four strands with which to tie a diamond knot, which can be doubled. This is a little tricky only because you have a lot of line to pull through the various tucks, but it makes a neat job.

❖ After the diamond knot, make up the main part of the lead with four-strand round sennit, breaking the plainness with the odd Matthew Walker or diamond knot, should you fancy. Make the four-strand round sennit overlong, as it is difficult to continue the sennit if you stop and then decide to make it longer. If you want to add some more variation, finish the four-strand round sennit with a diamond knot, then make about 100mm of four-strand crown sennit.

❖ When you are happy with the length, make a temporary seizing round all four strands with a constrictor knot and, using the two shorter ends as the core, continue with a length of Portuguese flat sennit, long enough to form a comfortable handle loop.

❖ Finish off by tucking the ends through the four-strand sennit where it changes to the Portuguese sennit and use the ends to make the extended diamond knot to cover the join.

❖ Walk your sea dog with pride or, perhaps, allow your sea dog to walk you with pride!

Jib SHACKLE

When crawling about on the foredeck with the jib flapping around your head the last thing you want is a lump of metal trying to hit you as well. How the jib sheets are fixed to the jib is quite important. This rope jib shackle is a safe substitute for the metal shackle so often used. I call it a Dutchman's jib shackle because that is what Brightlingsea sailmaker James Lawrence called it when I first spotted this useful arrangement of lanyard knot, double crown and seizing.

We get many a Dutch visitor to the east coast of England and I guess it was first introduced to our region by one such visitor. There are other variations using the boatswain's whistle lanyard knot (see page 27) which are sometimes made with braided Dyneema/ Spectra, but this version of the lanyard knot, based on a wall knot with a double crown finish, gives a good wide flat button. This lanyard knot was used as the stopper knot on the lanyard that is reeved through the deadeyes to set up standing rigging.

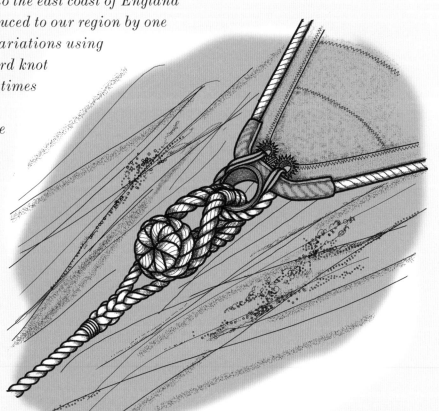

MATERIALS

* 1m of 10mm three-strand rope
* A few metres of whipping twine

KNOTS USED

* Lanyard knot
* Double crown – see page 36
* Flat seizing – see page 43

METHOD

❖ Middle the rope and put on a flat seizing about 220mm from the bight. Unlay the ends and make a wall knot with the six strands, making the extra tuck with each end as shown in the illustration.

❖ Carefully work fairly tight, but not too tight, as the ends now have to be crowned and tucked down the middle in the same way we finish the star knot (see page 35), making a double crown knot.

❖ If you have a hot knife or even a heated hacksaw blade, trim the ends close to the back of the knot. Make another flat seizing to make a loop just big enough to allow the knot to be 'buttoned' through. You can now use this instead of that wicked metal shackle.

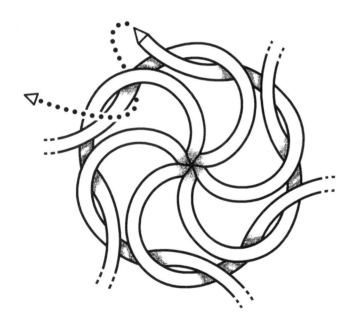

Tuck all strands as shown

The finished jib shackle

Rope Mats

Things you can do to MATS

While rope mats can be pulled up tightly and used just as they are, there are some other ways to help them keep their shape and perform better (beware, though, these methods can also have their downsides):

- The outer rows of the mat can be sewn in place using a sail or packing needle, quite a time-consuming job, but may well be useful on some designs.
- If you are making your mats into coasters or table mats, you may stiffen them with a coating of acrylic or PVA-based glues or varnishes. I have mentioned this before for sealing other types of ropework (see pages 15-16, 83, 100), but do check how the varnish or glue reacts with the material you are using.
- A rope mat can have clear sealant, the type used to seal joins round baths or windows, smeared over the back, which helps to keep the various layers of rope in place and gives a bit of a non-slip to the back. This, of course, means that the mat is now non-reversible.
- Even if you leave the mat without any additional treatment, but it is to sit on a very smooth or shiny surface, such as a polished floor, you may find that it pays to put a bit of anti-slip material under it. This material is usually sold either to go under conventional rugs to stop them slipping, or to act as an anti-slip mat itself on a table, dashboard or shelf of a boat, car or caravan.
- If the mat uses a great deal of material and is always followed round on the same side throughout the mat, consider making it in two colours, as this cuts down the amount of material needed to be pulled through, thus making the job quicker.

∾ MAKING A PIN BOARD ∾

It can be very useful to use a pin board to pin out a complex mat. I use T pins, but other push pins will work as well. The board can be made from soft pulp insulating board; sometimes a builders' yard will have a damaged board that can be bought much cheaper than a full board and you only need a modest amount.

There are problems, however: after much use this board has a tendency to break down, covering you in fibre; and a pin can be thrust right through and either stick into your leg, if you are working on your lap, or damage a table if you are working on a table.

Kaj Lund, that skilled mat maker, recommended gluing a piece of hardboard to the back of the pulp board and then coating the whole board with a couple of coats of shellac. This gives the board a much longer life, stops pins being pushed right through and helps immensely when pinning out the pattern of a complex mat. A board treated this way is also good to pin out and work on square knotting or macramé.

Flat three-lead, four-bight
TURK'S HEAD MAT

 *The carrick bend knot structure is the basis of many pleasing knots, as can be seen on pages 27, 135. Tied flat in a single piece of line and bringing one end round to follow the other back through the structure creates a delightful little mat design. This is actually a flattened three-lead, four -bight Turk's head. It is also the logo of the International Guild of Knot Tyers (IGKT), a knot signifying the four points of the compass, all joined together in a knot. Many IGKT members tie it in very small stuff to make their own badge.*

Tied in 4mm and followed round four times makes a very small drink's mat. It must be said that tied in bigger stuff it becomes a bit cumbersome; if you want a bigger mat there are many others in this book that are well worth tying and may prove better for your purpose.

MATERIALS

* 450mm of 2mm braid, followed round twice, will make a 25mm diameter badge

* 2.1m of 4mm, followed four times round, makes a drink's mat of about 10cm diameter

KNOTS USED

* Three-lead, four-bight Turk's head

* If using three-strand rope, side splice finish - see page 147 - or flat seizing - see page 43 - or even gluing if you use fine material

METHOD

❖ Lay out the line as shown, making sure that the overs and unders correspond and are locked in place by taking the line under, over, under, over, and round to the start, as in the dotted line.

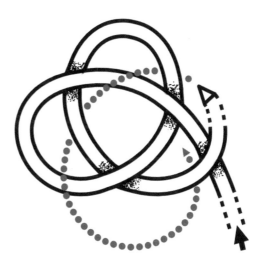

Starting the three-lead, four-bight Turk's head

❖ Follow round on the inside to double or treble the mat. Finish with the appropriate finish for the rope used. When very small line is used, it may be better to glue or melt (for synthetic materials), with the join on the hidden side of the little 'mat'. This will certainly not matter if the finished item is to be glued to some kind of badge pin from a jewellery supply company.

Ocean and prolong *mats*

Rope mats are very satisfying to make, be they small for a glass to sit on, bigger to go under a plate or bigger still to wipe shoes on before coming on to a boat or into a house. Door mats are a useful way of using worn-out sheets or halyards or even lifeboat falls. Be warned that mats use a lot more rope than you would expect. It is worth keeping a note of the amount of rope that has gone into a particular mat for later reference.

The ocean and prolong mats are the most common of rope mats and are both constructed in the same manner; the only difference is that one starts from an overhand knot and the other from a carrick bend. The overhand knot start gives a mat with three bights on its side, while the carrick bend start gives a mat with four bights to the side.

In both cases, they can be lengthened by repeating the basic twist and tuck process used to start them – each time this is done the mat gets another three bights to its side.

As with all flat knot mats, you make the initial knot and then follow round to double, triple, quadruple or even go as many as six times round. If, when you have made your mat you find it a bit on the small side, then it is possible to increase the whole by coiling rope round the outside of the mat and sewing the turns together.

MATERIALS

* 650mm x 400mm ocean mat, four times round, uses 25m of 14mm rope

* 600mm x 340mm ocean mat, three times round, uses 14m of 18mm rope

* 800mm x 400mm prolong mat, four times round, uses 30m of 14mm

* 1000m x 450mm prolong mat, four times round, uses 29m of 24mm rope

KNOTS USED

* Overhand knot

* Carrick bend

* Side splice finish - see page 147 - or flat seizing - see page 43

METHOD

❖ In the middle of the rope, tie either an overhand knot or a carrick bend with the ends on the same side (sometimes called the Josephine knot).

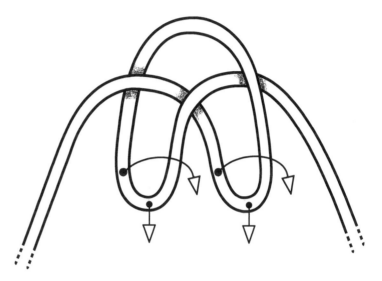

Overhand knot start for ocean mat

Carrick bend: From this start the prolong mat can be made in the same way as the ocean mat

❖ Pull down a pair of loops and twist and overlay as shown below, then bring down first one end of the rope and then the other, interweaving to complete the design.

❖ The knot can then be followed round in both directions as many times as you like or as the rope allows.

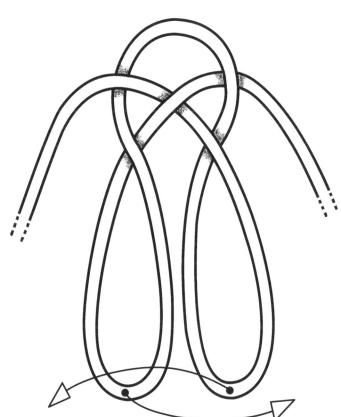

Pull down a pair of loops and twist and overlay like this

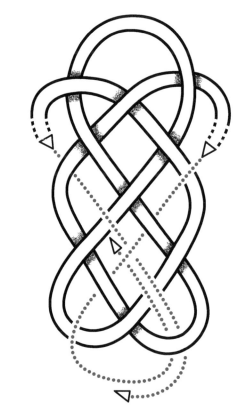

Now follow round as many times as required

❖ When you've got the mat to the rough size and shape, it is then time to work any slack or irregularity out; do this a bit at a time as it is very difficult to work slack back into a mat that has become too tight.

THUMP *mat*

👉 *A deck-mounted block has an annoying habit of thumping on the deck every time the rope running through it slackens at all, doing the deck no good, nor the nerves of those on board. By putting a rope mat over the eyebolt to which the block is attached, so making a cushion beneath the block, helps a great deal to deaden the noise, protects the deck from chafe and looks very smart. I first saw this fairly simple thump mat in Hervey Garrett Smith's delightful book* Marlinspike Sailor *and have made it both as a thump mat and as a generously sized drink's mat. In many ways it is related to the kringle mat on page 140.*

MATERIALS

* 6m of 6mm line, four times round, makes a small thump mat of 200mm diameter

* 4m of 4mm, four times round, makes a drink's size thump mat of 120mm diameter

* 17m of 10mm, five times round, makes a big thump mat of 430mm diameter

KNOTS USED

* Thump mat over-under pattern

* Side splice finish - see page 147 - or flat seizing - see page 43

METHOD

❖ Start near the middle of your line and make the initial loop with its crossings. Take the end on the right-hand side and make another loop, being careful to pass over two parts of the initial loop and only tuck under once, as shown with red dots in the diagram below; with the other end do much the same, but make sure that the end goes under, under, over, under, over. Note that there will be a part of the mat that does not yet have a complete over, under pattern structure.

❖ To complete, take the right-hand end and go over, under, over, under and bring it to mate with the left-hand end. You now should have a complete design with a full over, under structure.

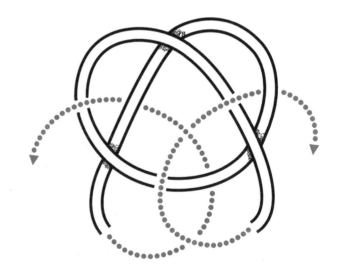

Start

Over-under pattern

❖ Make sure that the design is neat and balanced before starting to follow round the design the number of times you would like. You can use both ends to do this. As always it helps to make the initial mat a little loose and tighten up afterwards.

❖ To finish, seize or, if using three-strand rope, use the side splice finish.

KRINGLE *mat*

☞ *Here is a mat I first found in Kaj Lund's book,* Måtter og Rosetter *(Mats and Rosettes). It consists of a series of interlinked knots that bear a similarity to the shop sign used in Denmark to denote a cake shop. This sign is in the form of the cake or biscuit called a 'kringle', hence the name that Kaj Lund gave it. It can be tied with any number of these knots interlinked; I prefer five, but if you want to use the mat as a thump mat then six knots will give a slightly bigger hole in the middle to go round the eyebolt taking the block.*

A mat made with five knots tripled in 3mm line makes an ideal mat for a coffee cup; the same mat in 6mm would be ideal for the teapot to stand on, while made in 10mm or 12mm rope and followed round five times you would have a useful mat for the bottom of the companionway steps, giving a modest yacht a touch of class.

By making a long series of interlinked knots and opening out the centre, the whole resulting knot can be arranged as an alternative to a Turk's head to decorate a tiller or such like.

MATERIALS

✳ 4m of 3mm cord will make a
five-knot mat followed round
three times of about 100mm
in diameter

✳ 6.5m of 6mm rope will make a
five-knot mat followed three
times round of about 180mm
diameter

✳ 37m of 10mm rope will make
a five-knot mat followed
round five times of about
600mm in diameter

KNOTS USED

✳ Kringle mat pattern

✳ Flat seizing - see page 43
- or side splice finish - see
page 147

METHOD

❖ Starting somewhere near the middle of the rope make the initial knot
form. You may wish to pin the cord in place, but I find I can hold it in
position with the flat of my hand. Bring the rope round and make the
second knot, inter-linking it with the first. Carry on until you get to the fifth
knot, which should inter-link to complete the circle.

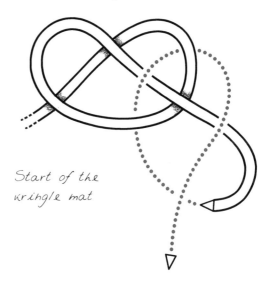

Start of the
kringle mat

Follow round as many
times as required

❖ Make the knots even and neat and follow round first,
with one end of the rope and then in the other direction
with the other end. When the required number of passes
have been made, the mat should be worked to a neat and
even form, working out any slack a bit at a time. It is much
easier to work slack out of a loose mat than it is to work a
bit of slack back into a tight mat.

❖ You may find that a gentle thump with a mallet will help
to flatten and even out the mat. When your mat is how
you wish it to be, finish the ends off at the back by either
side splicing or seizing.

HITCHED OVAL *mat*

☞ *This mat is one of a number based on interwoven half hitches. It uses five half hitches, which are first interwoven and locked into place by three transverse passes. It is quite quick to tie and makes up as a very slightly asymmetrical oval shape. This mat is quite complicated, but a simpler one could be made using just three interwoven hitches.*

The hitched mat has a whole different feel to the ocean plait and prolonged knot mats. You need to take care when working the mat up tight, as rope in the transverse turns that link the hitches goes from inside to outside. It will make a fine doormat in 10mm, yet would be equally at home as a table mat if made in 6mm.

METHOD

❖ The mat should first be made big and loose, and afterwards tightened into the final size.

❖ In the middle of the rope, create five half hitches and interweave them as you make them. This will give you the base structure of the mat.

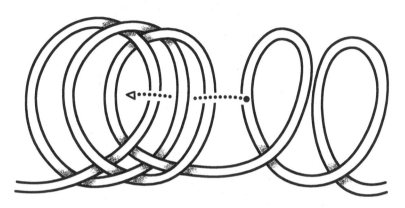

Interweave the hitches

❖ Make sure that where the outer two hitches overlap in the middle is as shown below.

Note how the hitches overlap in the middle

❖ With the right-hand working end, carefully follow the overs and unders, first to the left of the mat and then back.

❖ Finally with the left-hand working end, weave over and under, locking all in place. The basic layout of the mat is now made.

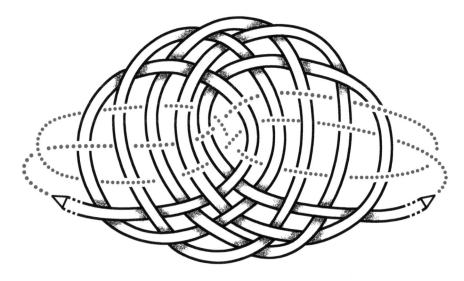

Carefully pass one end at a time through the hitches

❖ Work it into a fairly symmetrical shape and follow the design round three, four or five times, as you wish. You may not be able to complete your full number of passes with the mat in its oversized state, so gently tighten the whole thing, working slack out to each working end, thus giving yourself more line to complete your passes. Keep repeating this up until you have a perfect mat.

❖ Finish by either side splicing or flat seizing the ends.

OBLONG *deck mat*

☞ If you have the time and the material, this makes a very fine mat to collect any shore-side dirt before visitors board your boat. At home it makes a handsome door mat that will give years of use. I find that 10mm rope gives a good balance between cost, size and time in making, but do use whatever material you can lay your hands on.

If the rope is three-stranded it is possible to make a very neat mat side splice that is almost invisible after a little use and will allow you to turn the mat over to even out the wear.

Tied in 6mm, you can make a place mat for the galley table.

METHOD

❖ Divide your rope into two equal parts, neatly hanking each half. With one hank or bundle, lay out the design on the floor if it is door mat-sized, or on a table if it is to be a table mat. You will need to keep a close eye on the various 'overs' and 'unders' as they do not follow any logical pattern until the final pass that will lock the whole design.

❖ This initial layout should be a lot bigger than the finished size so that you may pass a whole bundle of line over and under rather than pulling the best part of twenty metres of rope as a single length through each time.

❖ After the initial knot has been tied, follow round until the rope runs out, then tighten the mat up a little.

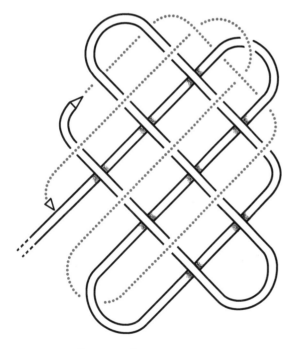

Start of the pattern

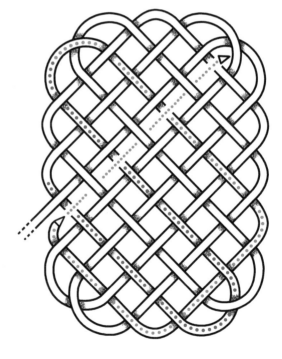

Follow round as many times as required

❖ It is not easy to keep the design even at this stage, as the rope goes first inside, then outside as it follows the path round the mat. Keep on working the mat into shape and following round with the slack that you build up.

❖ When you have gone round five times, you can work any slack or deformity out and finish off with the mat side splice if using three-strand rope or seize the two ends.

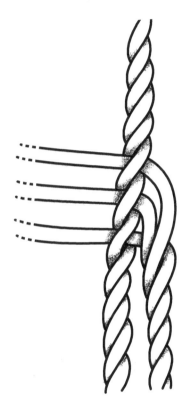

Start of the side splice finish

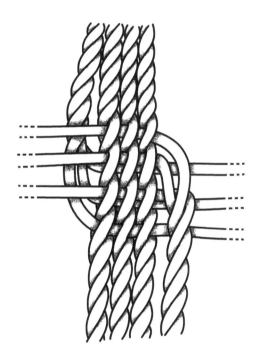

The complete side splice finish to the mat; work tight

❖ Do make sure that the mat is laid out correctly, good and fair, before being put to use. If one of the strands is out of place and repeatedly trodden down it is very difficult to correct later.

Mat designs that can be
GROWN BIGGER

The designs for these two mats are such that they can be grown, starting with a very simple mat design which, by a series of parallel tucks, can be made bigger and more complex; all this before you double or triple the design by following round in the usual manner.

The first mat is almost square, with sides that have but one bight or loop difference. This gives a wide range of achievable designs, from a very simple mat with two bights on one side and three on the other (2 x 3), which can be grown or expanded to 3 x 4, 4 x 5, 5 x 6 and so on. With the larger number of bights the single bight difference is barely noticeable and, by squashing it slightly, it can be made to fit a true square.

The second mat is long and thin. The design starts as a two bight by five bight (2 x 5) and can then be expanded to 3 x 7, 4 x 9, 5 x 11 and so on. This design can be useful where a long narrow mat is needed to fit a narrow space, or perhaps to go on a narrow step, in which case make sure that it is firmly fixed to the step with plenty of nails so that it does not slip.

ALMOST SQUARE MAT
METHOD

❖ Starting with an overhand knot opened up, take end A over, under, over, under, to join up with end B, to make the basic 2 x 3 mat.

❖ From this base, take end A over B and follow back, parallel to the line ending B and turn back at the corner, returning over, under, over, under, over, to join up with end B again. This should give a complete over-under patterned mat with three bights on the short side and four on the longer.

❖ To make this mat into a 4 x 5 bight mat, this time take end B over A and run back parallel to the line ending A, turn again at the corner and return to lock the over-under design. By following this approach, first with one end and then with the other, the mat can be developed or grown to the required number of bights.

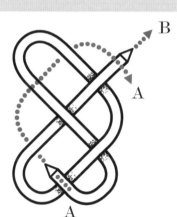
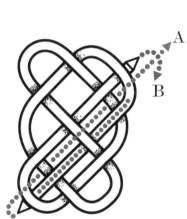
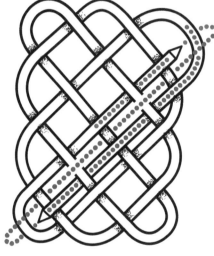

Starting and growing the almost square mat

❖ As you 'grow it', there is a tendency for the mat to become more diamond-shaped than square, so work some line into the tighter corners and square the whole thing up as you go. With the larger numbers of bights on the sides it should be possible to tweak the whole layout almost to a square.

MATERIALS

✱ 25m of 8mm rope, three times round, makes up a 3 x 7 bight mat sized about 500mm x 200mm.

KNOTS USED

✱ 2 x 5 bight mat pattern

✱ 3 x 7 bight mat pattern

LONG AND THIN MAT
METHOD

❖ Start by laying out the line loosely as shown below, bringing end A round under, over and, turning back, go under, over, under itself, then over. This starts to make one end of this mat. Continue with end A over, under, turn and come back over, under, over itself and under B. This gives the basic 2 x 5 bight mat.

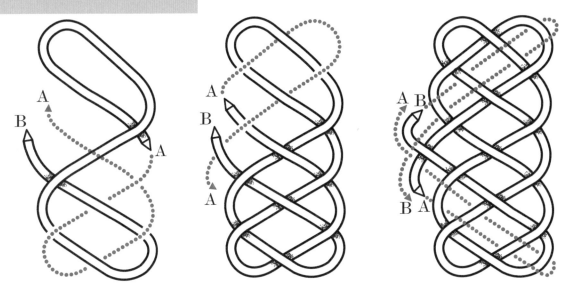

Starting and growing the long and thin mat

❖ To expand the 2 x 5 bight mat to a 3 x 7 bight mat, each end has to weave to one corner, turn back on itself and return, completing the over-under weave. I trust that the diagram above makes this clear, as the principle is very similar to that used on the almost square mat, but this time each end of the mat has to be expanded.

❖ Taking the 3 x 7 bight as a base, it can be expanded using the same system to a 4 x 9 bight and so on, as you wish.

❖ As you 'grow it', there is a tendency for two of the mat's corners to be more pointed, so work some line into the tighter corners and square the whole thing up as you go.

MATERIALS

For single cross mat:

✳ 36m of 12mm, five times round, makes up a mat sized about 710mm x 510mm

✳ 33m of 10mm five times round makes up a mat sized about 660mm x 480mm

✳ 20m of 7mm five times round makes up 585mm x 380mm

KNOTS USED

✳ Cross pattern

✳ Side splice finish – see page 147 – or flat seizing – see page 43

CROSS AND DOUBLE CROSS MAT

Here are a couple of oval, curvy mats with some open parts, which give a slightly different effect to the very solid over-under designs of many of the mats that I have made. You can decide just how open you make the side loops. I would suggest, if it is being used as a door mat, that they are pulled in fairly tight so as not to catch the heel of a shoe; perhaps the double cross mat would be the better of the two. The single version can look good as a table mat. Just how tight you make your mat will affect the amount of material used.

METHOD

❖ Start near the middle of the rope, laying it out as shown below. Note how the rope locks one part of the cross but leaves other bights or loops to be locked in place as you follow the path, completing the overall pattern as shown below.

❖ Double check that all overs and unders are correct before you start to follow round the pattern, doubling, trebling, etc., using both ends of the rope.

❖ Tighten and shape, finishing in the most appropriate manner for the cordage you have used.

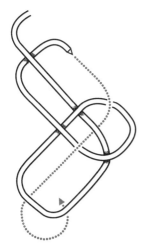

Start

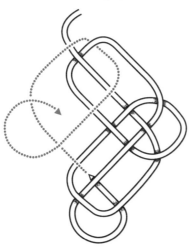

Second stage

Tucks to complete design

MATERIALS

* 20m of 7mm rope, five times round, makes up a mat sized about 405mm x 330mm.

* 40m of 10mm rope, six times round, makes up a mat sized about 685mm x 535mm.

KNOTS USED

* Double cross pattern

* Side splice finish - see page 147 - or flat seizing - see page 43

❖ As with the single cross mat, start near the middle of the rope, laying it out as shown below; note how the rope only goes over once. Follow the path shown, which locks one end of the mat, leaving the rest of the pattern to be completed as shown.

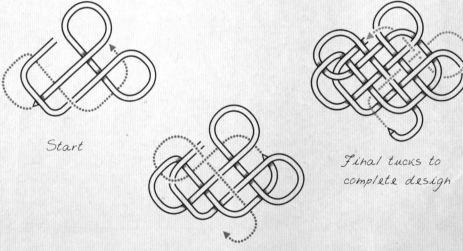

Start

Second stage

Final tucks to complete design

❖ Do double check that all overs and unders are correct before you start to follow round the pattern doubling, trebling, etc., using both ends of the rope. Tighten and shape, finishing in the most appropriate manner for the cordage you have used.

Oblong POINTED MAT

☞ *It was 1972 and my wife and I were exploring the old harbour in Copenhagen. There was a traditional ships chandler's that had in its window the usual pieces of boat fittings, but also a number of examples of sailors' ropework, a delight and inspiration to the aspiring ropeworker. Round the corner was a bookshop and, hoping that being in such a nautical part of the city there may be some interesting books that might help me gain knowledge and techniques, I went in.*

To my surprise, there I found three splendid books full of fresh ideas, all by an author who until then was unknown to me, Kaj Lund: Knob og Splejs *(Knots and Splices),* Tovvaerks Kunst *(Ropework Art) and* Måtter og Rosetter *(Mats and Rosettes). The fact that the words were in Danish did not matter to me, the pictures spoke in English.*

I bought all three and, in the mat book, saw a fine-looking mat that would make a gift for our host. So, back I went to the ship's chandler's and bought thirty metres of 16mm manila, which I took back to our friend's house and made up into a door mat. This is the mat I made.

MATERIALS

✱ 30m of 16mm rope, three times round, will make a modest doormat sized about 610mm x 480mm

✱ 42m of 16mm rope, four times round, will make a mat sized about 710mm x 535mm

✱ 10m of 6mm rope, three times round, will make a mat sized about 302mm x 205mm

KNOTS USED

✱ Oblong pointed mat pattern

✱ Side splice finish - see page 147 - or flat seizing - see page 43

METHOD

❖ Heavy rope tends to be stiffer so if you are using 16mm rope, you will find that it should bend and hold the curves quite easily. Lay out the rope as shown below, following round the dotted line; some parts of the mat will soon get locked in place. Complete the mat by continuing with the design as shown, until you reach the starting point.

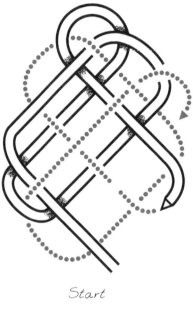

Start

Final tucks to complete design

❖ Check that all overs and unders are correct, before proceeding to double and treble as you wish.

❖ Finish in the most appropriate manner that suits you and the cordage used.

LARGE ROUND MAT *with six hitches on the outside*

Here is another mat from Kaj Lund, with six loops or hitches round the outside. I am not sure if Kaj Lund ever saw George Bain's book Celtic Art, but it is closely related to a Pictish circular design found on a stone slab at Hilton of Cadboll in Easter Ross, Scotland. I am more inclined to think that Kaj Lund developed his design from the more complex circular mat with twelve loops illustrated in Jens Kusk Jensen's Haandbog i Praktisk Sømandsskab (see page 158).

This mat needs a bit of concentration when making the first pass, but once the basic design has been formed in a single strand and the over-under pattern has been checked, following it round is quite simple, as there is none of that annoying problem of the line first going inside and then outside, which can distort the symmetry when tightening.

MATERIALS

✳ 45m of 20mm rope, four times round, makes up a mat 700mm in diameter

✳ 30m of 7mm rope, four times round, makes up a mat about 500mm in diameter

✳ 11m of 4mm rope, three times round, makes up a mat about 200mm in diameter

✳ 11m of 2mm cord, four times round, makes up a mat about 140mm in diameter

KNOTS USED

✳ Round mat pattern

✳ Side splice finish - see page 147 - or flat seizing - see page 43

METHOD

❖ As usual, start somewhere near the middle of the rope and make the series of small hitches and one large hitch. Keep a close watch on how the hitches are made and that the large hitch stays under the small hitches, as shown below

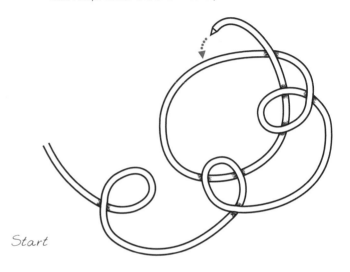

Start

❖ Carry on making a series of three small hitches and one large hitch as shown below; note that, as you make the big hitch, it locks quite a number of crossings.

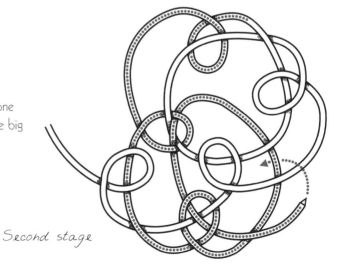

Second stage

❖ Complete the mat with another series of three small hitches and one large hitch; this time the first two small hitches are round earlier crossings and the large hitch or loop finishes off the whole under-over design.

Final tucks to complete design

❖ Check that all is correct before proceeding to double and treble etc. and working to shape.

❖ Finish in whatever manner works for you and your cordage.

JENS JENSEN'S BIG ROUND MAT *with twelve hitches on the outside*

👉 *The Danish sea captain Jens Kusk Jensen (1866–1936) wrote and illustrated an interesting work on seamanship,* Haandbog i Praktisk Sømandsskab, *first published in 1901. This book had several reprints and facsimiles. The section on practical ropework and rigging is full of interesting techniques and designs, based on his long years at sea; many are not shown elsewhere.*

One such design is this mat, which took him many years to be able to make from a single line. I suspect that the idea for this type of design originated in a stone carving somewhere in Denmark, as I am certain that Captain Jensen never saw the Hilton of Cadboll stone in Scotland, on which is carved this exact design.

While it is a very complex series of interlaced loops or hitches, if care is taken to follow the design, a handsome mat can be made. First try making the large round mat with six hitches on the outside on page 155 to get the general understanding as to how these sorts of mats work.

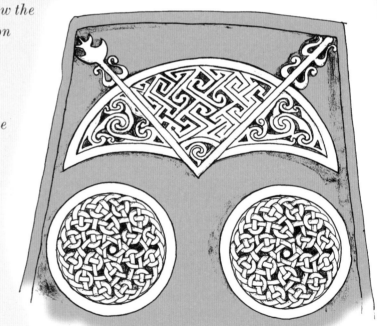

MATERIALS

* 65m of 6mm, four times round, makes up a mat 650mm in diameter

KNOTS USED

* Jens Jensen round mat pattern
* Side splice finish - see page 147 - or flat seizing - see page 43

METHOD

❖ This is a complex mat that needs careful attention to detail. You can try copying it and blowing it up to a large scale. Colour helps to give the structure and see where you are going and where you have been.

❖ You can start in the middle of your rope, but as there are so many tucks to be made, it may be easier to start with a third of the rope so there is less rope to tuck when locking crossing points.

❖ Do keep checking that earlier loops are still in place, as they can easily be displaced and then you are in trouble. Pinning out on a board can help or holding the crossing points with clips can also assist.

❖ Take it slowly and gradually follow round the design, using the coloured diagram shown below. It can help to mark the rope every now and then with a piece of masking tape with the colour written on it so that you can see where you are going in laying out the design against the diagram.

❖ When you think you have completed the pattern, double check that all crossings are right before following round.

❖ Finish in the way that suits the material and you best.

❖ This is a tricky mat to make, but one thing in its favour is that, when it comes to following round, the next pass always passes on the same side, either on the inside, if that is how you start to follow round, or on the outside. This makes it slightly easier to keep the shape. If you wish you can use two colours or types of rope.

The complete design

Rounded corner LARGE COMPLEX RECTANGULAR MAT

☞ *Skip Pennock of Maryland is a genius at designing all types of flat knot interweave from fishes to hearts and crosses and a couple of full alphabets of letters, together with a good few mats. If this sort of thing excites you seek out a copy of his book* Decorative Woven Flat Knots, *published by the International Guild of Knot Tyers.*

Here is an example of one of his designs. Liz, my wife, took her time and made this for a local yachtsman. Sadly it was washed overboard and she had to make another one; this time when it was finished she left one end coming out at the side as a lanyard so that it could be attached to the boat. We hope it is still in use today. This is not a mat for the faint-hearted, it is a challenge, but a rewarding mat is the result.

METHOD

❖ This mat needs plenty of attention. As usual, start in the middle of your rope; it may well help to pin down the line where it crosses another.

❖ Take your time. Liz finds it easier to colour parts of the design so that she can see where she is going. Getting the design photocopied and blown up in scale can also help. When Skip makes his drawings he puts in marks for pins, to help control the shape.

❖ Be absolutely certain that you have a complete over-under design before following round.

❖ Make it up loosely as it will be much easier to follow round. You can work it tighter later; as usual, a number of tightenings are better than too much tightening to start with.

❖ There will be a good few hours' work to make and finish this mat, but it is worth it. Good luck.

The complete design

SENNIT *mats*

☞ *In the past seafarers wasted nothing, especially rope. Old rope past its best was often cut up into short lengths called junk; the rope was untwisted and the best yarns were drawn from the strands. These yarns were either tied together and then twisted together to make twice-laid rope, or plaited together to make sennit.*

The sennit could be used for everyday tying or binding; it could also be used to make rope mats known as sennit mats. The sennit was made and then stitched together on its side, usually in a spiral, with a series of curlicues or mini coils to speed the growth of the mat and to give an element of decoration, as shown below.

Various styles of curlicue

❖ Sometimes the mat was started at the centre with a flat Turk's head mat such as on page 132, made from the sennit. Exactly which sennit was used was a matter of choice, the most basic being three-strand sennit, like a basic hair plait, as shown below, either with single strands, which tends to be a bit thin, or with pairs, 3 x 2 or even 3 x 3.

Three-strand sennit, like a basic hair plait

❖ There are also other sennits that work well; a five-strand or a seven-strand flat sennit. Both are shown below.

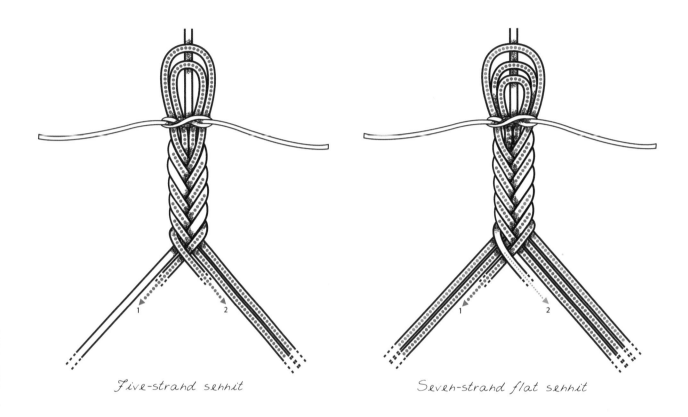

Five-strand sennit

Seven-strand flat sennit

❖ Making these mats takes a lot of time, but they are an ideal way to use up yarns drawn from old rope, or offcuts of new rope. Farmer's baler twine or even string will work just as well.

❖ There are no set patterns or rules; your imagination is king, but you will need plenty of yarns and plenty of time, so it may be a good idea to first make a small table mat.

❖ From my researches, I have found that sennit mats were quite common in the homes of seafarers, but as they tended to serve a very utilitarian task, they would be worn out and thrown away, leaving little evidence. By making one you will be reviving a piece of history.

METHOD

❖ Depending on which sennit you choose to make, fold over some yarns so that the tails are of differing lengths and tie in an extra one so that you are working with an odd number of yarns (or pairs or threes if making the very simple three-strand sennit).

❖ I usually prefer to work with seven yarns, as this makes a good thick mat; although, of course, the five-strand sennit grows quicker, and the three-strand sennit, be it single, pairs or triples, is perhaps the easiest to start with. Be bold and try the five- or seven-strand sennit.

❖ To make the sennit, the basic rule is that on one side you have an odd number of yarns, the other even. Take the outer yarn on the odd side and bring it across to the centre by the even side, thus making the even side into an odd number.

❖ Now take the outer yarn on what is now the odd number across to the middle, and keep repeating odd outer to the middle.

❖ When a yarn gets short, twist a new yarn round it and carefully bring it across and hold in place and carry on as before; the twist should be held in place by the later plaited yarns.

❖ Try to keep the joins spaced out. The hairy tails can be trimmed afterwards.

❖ Make up a good length of sennit and use a clothes peg to stop the sennit unravelling before starting to coil it on edge and sewing together, trying to hide the stitches.

❖ I like to use a sail needle or small packing needle; if your sennit is very tight you may need to use a sailmaker palm to help push the needle through, but this is not always necessary. When sewing together, I try to push the needle through not just the sennit it is next to, but to catch a second or third row as well, to ensure a good tight mat.

❖ Making curlicues, little spirals or fold-backs will make the mat grow quicker. As I have said, there are no set patterns, but there are a few examples illustrated.

❖ It is best to make up plenty of sennit and then pin in the first row of decorative details, making sure you evenly distribute them round the mat.

❖ One word of warning: if you are making curlicues, make them quite bold, as there is a tendency for them to close up when you add the outer rows of sennit.

SHEILA's *star mat*

☞ *A friend of mine had spent four years carefully restoring Sheila, a 25ft Albert Strange designed yawl, built in 1905.*

When he came to sail her, he had one problem: there was a slippery 400mm square hatch cover in the cockpit. So he asked me to make a rope mat for it, to give a good foothold. The mat also had to include a window to frame an eight-pointed star carved in the middle of the cover.

I suggested making the mat a star shape, and this was seized upon as being just the thing, as the star motif was already repeated elsewhere on the yacht. I thought it would not be too hard to find a suitable star mat in Matter og Rosetter *by Kai Lund, but there was nothing there that included a hole in the middle to show the carving. Now, if I had made a square mat, I would have based it on the prolong knot, so I set about trying to draw something star-shaped using prolong knots for the long arms and ocean plaits for the short arms of the star. Drawing these first and linking them, I found a mat and, best of all, a mat that could be tied from one piece of line. This was to be Sheila's star mat. (It would have been possible to have used the same technique to make a mat with six points and a smaller centre.)*

MATERIALS

* 60m of 4mm braid for the mat followed round 4 times makes up approx 400mm square

KNOTS USED

* The Star Mat diagrams 1, 2 and 3

* If tied in braided material use flat seizing - see page 43

* If tied in 3 strand cordage use the side splice finish - see page 147

Start the pattern from the middle

METHOD

❖ A mat as complex as this needs some help to get the design right. This may be one of the instances when it is worth photocopying the diagram above and enlarging it to a size a little over that of the finished mat, even if this means a number of copies. Use the copy as a guide, working directly over the diagram. You will certainly need to use pins pushed into a board to hold the cord as you progress.

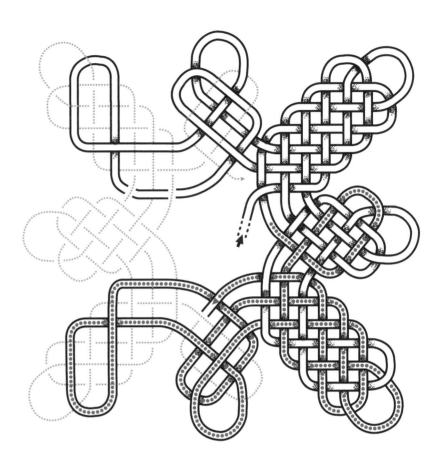

Continue to build up the points of the star

❖ As usual, start in the middle of the rope you are using, thus keeping the amount of rope to be tucked to a minimum. When the four passes have been made you will need to even out the points, making sure that the star is symmetrical. When you are using braided material, the finish should be with a flat seizing hidden under one of the crossing points, preferably near the middle. If you have used a 3 strand material, then the side splice finish is the neatest.

Finish off the complete pattern
and check that the under and
over sequence is correct before
doubling etc

FURTHER READING

For me books have always been a great source of knowledge and inspiration.

This is not a full bibliography of knot books but a selection of books that I think will help to expand on various areas of knotting and thus increase your versatility.

Some are now out of print, but it should be possible to find new or good second-hand copies online.

CW Ashley, *The Ashley Book of Knots*

G Budworth, *The Hamlyn Book of Knots: Ornamental and Useful*

CL Day and L Hoffman, *The Art of Knotting and Splicing*

R Edwards, *Knots Useful and Ornamental*

R Edwards, *Turk's-heads*

S Grainger, *Creative Ropecraft*

S Grainger, *Knotcraft*

R Graumont and J Hensel, *The Encyclopaedia of Knots and Fancy Rope Work*

PPO Harrison, *The Harrison Book of Knots*

F Hin, *The Colour Book of Knots*

C Jones, *The Fender Book*

L Popple, *Advanced Ropeworking*

D Pawson, *The Handbook of Knots*

D Pawson, *Knots Step by Step* (USA edition: *Knots, the complete visual guide*)

D Pawson, *The Pocket Guide to Knots and Splices*

D Pawson, *Sailors' Rope Mats from Yarns, Strands and Sennit*

S Pennock, *Decorative Woven Flat Knots*

L Philpott, *The Ultimate Book of Decorative Knots*

HG Smith, *The Marlinspike Sailor*

CL Spencer, *Knots, Splices and Fancy Work*

B Toss, *The Rigging Handbook*

Q Winch, *Nets and Knots*

Knotting Matters, the magazine of the International Guild of Knot Tyers

USEFUL SUPPLIERS

IN THE UK:

Classic Marine
Suffolk Yacht Harbour Ltd
Levington
Ipswich
Suffolk IP10 0LN
Tel: +44 (0)1394 380 390
Email: info@classicmarine.co.uk
Website: www.classicmarine.co.uk

KJK Ropeworks
Kevin Keatley Ltd
Tiverton Way
Tiverton Business Park
Tiverton
Devon EX16 6TG
Tel: +44 (0)1884 254 191
Fax: +44 (0)1884 250 460
Email: cords@kjkropeworks.co.uk
Website: www.cordsandropes.com

Rope Services UK
The Ropeworks
2 Market Place Industrial Estate
Houghton Le Spring DH5 8AW
Telephone: +44 (0)191 584 2709
Fax: +44 (0)191 460 6614
Mobile: 07711 245 494
Email: sales@ropeservices.co.uk
Website: www.ropeservicesuk.com

Tradline Rope and Fenders
Braunston Marina
Braunston
Daventry
Northamptonshire NN11 7JH
Tel: +44 (0)1788 891 761
E-mail: enquires@tradline.co.uk
Website: www.tradline.co.uk

IN THE USA:

Martin Combs
Tel: +1 (252) 335 7408
Email: roundturn@hotmail.com
Website: www.knotstuff.com

R&W Enterprises
39 Tarkiln Place
New Bedford
MA 02745
Tel: +1 (508) 997 1114/+1 (800) 260 8599
Fax: +1 (508) 997 9990
Email: info@rwrope.com
Website: www.rwrope.com

THE INTERNATIONAL GUILD OF KNOT TYERS

The International Guild of Knot Tyers was founded in 1982. It is a registered charity (No. 802153) with the declared object of 'the advancement of education by the study of the art, craft and science of knotting, past and present'. The Guild regularly publishes a magazine, *Knotting Matters*, that is sent to all members. There are now well over 1,100 members in more than 25 countries. Groups of members meet together both in small local meetings and in much larger international meetings.

Membership is open to all who have an interest in knot tying, be they highly skilled or just beginners.

For more information please see www.igkt.net or contact secretary@igkt.net.

ACKNOWLEDGEMENTS

This book would be nothing without the patience and creative input from the artists and designers Ann Norman, Tracy Saunders and Claudia Myatt, who turned my scribbles and bits of rope into such clear diagrams and illustrations, and Horst Friedrichs, whose atmospheric photos add a certain something to the overall feel of the book.

Thanks also to the editors at Adlard Coles Nautical, who believed in the idea of this book, and their designer who gave the book its special look.

Lastly for the support of Liz, my wife, who has worked with me for so many years and helps make my words make sense.

Any error that may be found is my responsibility.

CONVERSION TABLE

Approximate conversion, metric to imperial, for working with cordage

Remember: material sizes can vary from maker to maker; and rope measured under tension can get shorter and fatter when worked or measured slack.

ROPE DIAMETERS	
metric	**imperial**
2mm	$\frac{1}{16}$ inch
3mm	$\frac{1}{8}$ inch
4mm	$\frac{3}{16}$ inch
6mm	$\frac{1}{4}$ inch
8mm	$\frac{3}{8}$ inch
10mm	$\frac{3}{8}$ inch
12mm	$\frac{1}{2}$ inch
14mm	$\frac{5}{8}$ inch
16mm	$\frac{5}{8}$ inch
18mm	$\frac{3}{4}$ inch
20mm	$\frac{7}{8}$ inch
22mm	$\frac{7}{8}$ inch
24mm	1 inch
30mm	$1\frac{1}{4}$ inches
36mm	$1\frac{1}{2}$ inches
48mm	2 inches
54mm	$2\frac{1}{2}$ inches
72mm	3 inches
96mm	4 inches

LINEAR MEASUREMENTS	
metric	**imperial**
25mm	1 inch
50mm	2 inches
75mm	3 inches
125mm	5 inches
150mm	6 inches
200mm	8 inches
300mm	12 inches/1 foot
600mm	2 feet
900mm	3 feet
1000mm/1m	3 feet 3 inches
2m	6 feet 6 inches
3m	10 feet
4m	13 feet
5m	16 feet 6 inches
6m	20 feet
7m	23 feet
8m	26 feet
9m	30 feet
10m	33 feet
20m	66 feet
30m	100 feet

INDEX